Alice in the Palace

Alice
in the
Palace

Joe Reed

cover art by Michele Reed, drawn on the front of a card for Alice's dear friend Kenzie.

For Michele,
whose intense, active love for Alice was magnificent to watch
&
for my beloved children,
Natalie, Joe, Emily, Kylie, and Violet,
who loved and were loved by Alice, and whose faith, hope, and love make me the proudest dad ever.

Table of Contents

Preface

Of making many books there is no end

Ecclesiastes 12:12b

Heaven knows we probably don't need another book. But if there's no end to making them, perhaps no significant harm will come of making another, so I will add this droplet to the perpetual effusion produced by a wordy humanity. Who knows, perhaps these pages will even be beneficial to someone. So here we go.

This is a compilation of the record of my thoughts as we walked with our daughter Alice through her journey into the valley of the shadow of death. I wish I could say we also walked with her out of that valley, but it would be more accurate to say we handed her off to the Lord Jesus, who walked her out of it, leaving us to return home empty-handed. This is my telling of what that experience felt like and the thoughts going through my mind as we labored to understand the simultaneous truths of disease and death in a broken world and a God whose love is infinite and his abilities equally so, whose purposes can never be frustrated, and square them with the reality of the experience we endured.

When Alice was diagnosed with a terminal, incurable brain stem tumor, one of the challenges my wife and I faced was the pressure (mostly self-imposed, no doubt, but real nonetheless) to keep our concerned friends and family appropriately in the loop. For a couple of reasons, in this age of social media when communication to a global audience is the norm and almost expected, I decided to take this responsibility on myself. Besides, writing helps me process and clarify my thoughts and this exercise became quite helpful to me. Also, my position as a pastor put us in a somewhat visible position and I didn't want Michele to have to be any more public than she wanted to be, which isn't much.

Besides, I wanted to be the one fielding all the *"Oh your child has cancer – do this thing and it'll be all better"* bits of very well-intentioned but almost entirely unhelpful or counterproductive advice. Communicating a story via online channels is a bit more dialogue than simply writing articles in a magazine, what with comment boxes and all. Between Michele and I, I wanted to be the one telling Alice's story and engaging in the ensuing conversation. Not surprisingly, it's quite difficult to receive hope-filled solutions from those who really believe they are offering the answer we're really hoping might be found, all the while keeping in mind that in Alice's particular case, all of the hopeful things had been tried and proven to fail. As human beings, we really want to win. From the early days of Alice's case however, we mostly tried to prepare to lose in the best way possible.

Hope is a good thing, but a false hope can be a cruel thing, and one must carefully choose the rocks upon which his hope will be anchored in a storm such as we endured. I wanted to be at the forefront of fielding and handling all of this hope offered to us rather than burdening Michele with it, and I'm glad I was. I hope she was too.

As much as anything, and especially as our ordeal unfolded, these little chapters became a way for me to wrestle through, process, and express my unfolding thoughts about God's love, his plans, and his willingness to allow his children to walk down some incredibly unpleasant paths. I have known for some time through study of the Bible and observation that God sometimes asks His children to endure severe pain. This is a record of me learning that same truth through experience, and what it felts like, to me at least, in the process.

Thanks to everyone who walked down those dark roads with us, and especially those who encouraged me to arrange this in book form. Without your insistence, this would have never happened. Thanks to my children who really weren't that crazy about Dad opening up such a wide window into our troubled little world – we really are a pretty private family. But I'm incredibly proud of them and delight in showing off God's grace in our home. Thanks to Michele who read and approved everything I wrote before I posted it, and supported me every step of the way.

Thanks to my Dad for helping me edit many of the chapters. Even when only searching for typos and clumsy grammar, reliving some of these days is really not all that enjoyable, and I'm grateful for his help. All the remaining blunders are entirely my own fault. The teeth of my editorial comb are hardly fine.

The original articles along with comments from friends and family and strangers across the globe can be found at www.commonslaves.com.

Joe Reed
June 14, 2019

Alice: crazy beautiful, crazy hair

Chapter 1

Alice

*I*n various conversations around the dinner table over the last couple of months, my wife and I would occasionally discuss the fact that it seemed the "light" had gone out of our little girl's eyes.

This caught our attention, because Alice's smile, utilizing every part of her cute little face, could infamously light up a room of any size. Since she has seasonal allergy issues, we chalked it up to them, and did the whole Zyrtec, Allegra, Claritin thing, figuring one of them would clear it up.

Then she seemed a bit more unstable on her feet from time to time. Shaky might be a better word. Not much, just a little. Still our happy little girl, to be sure. Last Tuesday when I came home from work she met me at the front door, which, being a Daddy's girl she often did, and as we talked together, I noticed her eyes weren't quite tracking with each other. Not crossed, and not really a lazy eye, just not quite in alignment.

I mentioned this to Shelly, and she said she'd been thinking that same thing for a couple of days but figured it might just be her worrisome nature making things up. If I saw the same thing though, maybe we should get her checked out. Wednesday morning (Sept. 20) I brought her to see an LPN who suggested some additional allergy treatments, gave us a referral to an allergy and an eye specialist, and sent us home. In previous experience, it takes weeks or months to see a specialist, but when Shelly called, they had an appointment for Friday morning in Wyoming, MN.

We watched, Shelly worried, and when Friday morning came, we really only had one question for the allergy specialist: "Do allergies make eyes misalign?" Answer: No. We were given some additional allergy info, and we left. Proud of her for enduring several trips to the doctor and more than a little worried about what was going on, I took her to Target to buy her any teddy bear she wanted, and for once, I was hoping she'd pick the expensive one. She made a solid mid-range choice, and when asked his name a thousand times over the next two days always called him "Bear." Then we headed back home. On the way, we called the Pine City clinic once again, figuring we'd try to be seen by someone else, and were able to get an appointment for 3:00 that same afternoon.

As I sat in the waiting room with Violet, our sixth child and only four weeks old, Shelly accompanied Alice into the exam room. The Doctor took one look at her, and as the first medical professional to see in her eyes what we saw, said almost immediately, but with concern, "I don't know what this is." He ordered some blood to be drawn for lab tests. A nurse came to get me to help hold Alice while they drew blood. So Shelly and I switched places, and she returned to the waiting room to sit with Violet.

I sat holding Alice while two nurses worked on getting a needle in her arm to draw some blood. They missed the vein they were looking for the first time, and were just starting to make a second attempt, Alice making me so proud by the way she kept calm, when the Doctor walked back in the room and told them quite curtly and firmly to stop the process, pull the needle, abort the mission. Weird.

After the nurses left, the Doctor said to me, "I called down to Children's Hospital, and actually got a neurologist on the phone. He said bring her down. Take her to the ER."

"Now? It's Friday evening, wouldn't we go Monday?"

"We don't want to wait until Monday. I'll tell them you're coming."

Our oldest daughter Natalie was working at the Dairy Queen in town, so we made a quick stop to tell her our plans, swung home to grab an overnight bag (how my wife manages to gather up all the essentials in a matter of five hyper-stressed minutes is beyond me), kiss the other kids good-bye, and headed down to Minneapolis.

Thank the Lord for friends and family who dropped everything to care for the kids over the next couple of days. We've not had a request denied us, no matter how inconvenient it's been.

At the ER Alice went through a battery of little tests: Look at the light, watch my finger, push my hands, walk, jump, stand on one leg, etc. Shelly and I answered a zillion questions. The doctor in charge said her eyes weren't technically crossed, and in a moment where no medical people were in our room, we said to each other that his eyes seemed a little crossed just like hers. Probably this was nothing.

Little Alice, naturally shy, slowly warmed up to every one of the doctors and residents who came in and ran the same little tests with her. She must have followed fingers and looked at lights and touched this or that a thousand times. But at the end of a few hours, it sounded like they were sending us home.

But before they let us go, the ER Doctor made one more call to a neurologist, and when he returned from that call, his tone had changed. Now we were staying the night. She was going to get an MRI.

So they moved us "upstairs," got us settled in, and over the course of that Friday night it felt like she had to endure a million more "follow my finger, what's your bear's name, look at my nose, push on my hands," and blood pressure readings.

Shelly had about had it when Alice didn't finally get enough quiet time free from these tests to fall asleep until about midnight, only to be woke up yet again (and it's not easy for a sleeping Alice to wake up, as those who know her can testify!) to look at the light, squeeze fingers, etc.

The MRI happened about noon. Alice, exhausted, fell asleep long before they sedated her so she wouldn't wiggle while in the machine. For a long hour and a half, we sat in an empty waiting room, trying to eat, holding Violet, knowing nothing, while I mused aloud to Shelly that we might be just wasting everyone's time and money. She assured me we weren't, but I'm not sure if that helped or not.

As we sat there, a voice came over the intercom trying to be calm, but was clearly panicked: "Code 21, unit 1, code 21." Was that Alice? What's going on? I grabbed my phone and googled code 21, and actually found a code sheet from the University hospital. Code 21 is a potentially explosive situation, apparently something like a volatile patient about to go ballistic. Well that wasn't Alice. But it showed us how raw our nerves were.

Then the MRI was done, and we went back to sit in the sedation unit with Alice as she woke up, very slowly, in her Alice way. Then back to the hospital room to wait.

After an hour or two, a young man walked into our room and introduced himself as a neurological resident. He asked us a few questions, said something about "showing us the pictures," talked to Alice for a little bit, and then walked over to the computer. As he was taking us over to the other side of the room, he said, "They don't call in a neurologist to deliver good news." He said they'd found a tumor at the top of her brain stem. As he pulled up the scan of her head, I was looking at a little black dot wondering if that was it. He pointed to a massive white section, right in the middle of her brain. "This is a tumor. This white thing isn't supposed to be here. This is not good. It's basically inaccessible, we can't get to it."

Gulp. That thing was (and is still, at this point), gigantic. He talked us through the concept of lakes of fluid in the brain, and how the lakes drain down rivers, and this tumor, as it grows, will put pressure on the rivers (like squeezing a straw I suppose) until they eventually get blocked off entirely, which then builds up pressure in the brain and does all kinds of bad stuff. Then he explained how a child's brain is so "plastic" and developing so rapidly, it learns to develop around the tumor, and function with it in there. But at some point, the brain can't handle it anymore, and that's when you start to notice some of the symptoms. These things usually show up by the time a child is Alice's age.

He wasn't hopeless, but he wasn't hopeful. So far, I guess we can say the same for pretty much all the doctors we've talked with. The hospital's brain tumor specialist came to see us on Sunday morning, which to me was a testament of the gravity of the situation, since I don't think he typically works Sunday, and he talked to us a little bit about sending us home for a few days while they assembled a team to do a biopsy because, as he said, "I want to see this thing under my microscope."

He ran some of the same little tests – follow my finger, look here, squeeze this, push that – and said to the team that followed him into our room, (rather cryptically, to us) "I've seen what I needed to see," and was gone. But we liked him, he's the only one thus far to use the term "determine the path to recovery," which still rang a little hollow but we hope he knows what he's talking about.

An hour after he left, the hospital's chief neurosurgeon came to see us, a polite but clearly no-nonsense woman with strawberry blonde hair.[1] She introduced herself and her team and said, "You won't be needing us, as this is inoperable." Later we wondered why she ever came to see us, given that seemed to be what she came to tell us.

---

[1] Behind her back (since we're polite, respectable people!), and *mostly* joking, Michele and I came to refer to her as "the crabby doctor." This was the only time we saw her, however, and who knows what her name for us was behind our back. Turnabout is, after all, fair play.

I asked her, "What's the procedure for doing a biopsy?" I wanted to know how they get a needle in the middle of her brain to get the tissue. "Oh, we don't do biopsies on this kind of tumor. This is a gliomic tumor. We only do that if we don't know what it is, and we know what this one is."

That was news to me. I told her the previous doctor said he wanted to do one. "Oh, I see. We haven't talked and I thought I'd get here before him. Well, a biopsy will give us some specifics that may allow you to enroll in clinical trials and experimental treatments." Hardly comforting terms.

For a number of reasons I avoid googling medical questions, but because I wanted to try to get some idea of a prognosis, and the doctors had (and thus far have) carefully avoided giving us one (which I don't blame them for, as their information is still incomplete as I write), I checked out gliomic brain stem tumors. There are apparently two kinds, one is mean and nasty, and the other one is more docile and treatable. They only biopsy the docile kind. So, I figure the neurosurgeon is convinced this is one of the mean ones.

One of the resident neurologists came back in our room a few hours later to talk with us again and as I chatted with him about what the neurosurgeon had said and asking why we would or wouldn't do a biopsy, she said that the brain tumor doctor we had seen first had seen something just different enough in Alice's tumor that he wanted to get another look at it. I think that's hopeful. I asked her, "This feels hopeless, should we be hopeful?"

She said, "I'd stick with hopeful. And enjoy her for..." and then she kind of rescued that train of thought somehow, but I'll never remember how she did it.

My wife asked Pastor Ivan Fiske to come pray with us, and so on Saturday afternoon he did. After church on Sunday, Pastor Bob came from Lewis Lake, knelt on the floor beside her bed, and wept. God bless those dear men. Shelly and I cry, a lot. But we are enjoying Alice. We are amazed by the outpouring of affection and love from all corners of our little world. It's funny – we know God is sovereign, and if a sparrow doesn't fall without Him knowing about it, Alice doesn't have a tumor without Him knowing about it. But just when it seems like we should be angry with Him for not stopping it, or wonder why, of all people, it should be our Alice, we remember that He is our only real hope. So we look to the God who superintends tumors and say, "Oh God, help us trust your wisdom and grace."

I've often said the past few days, "Jesus loves the little children, but He loves them in strange ways." That's how I feel. But if I don't understand the strange ways, I do understand He loves Alice, and He loves us.

Thursday is biopsy day. We still won't have a prognosis for a couple of days while the pathologists do their thing. They are assembling the best they've got (and they've all been absolutely wonderful, and if I sound like I'm complaining, I'm not. There's just not a lot of "glad game" left in me right now), which is both a comfort and a concern. I wish Alice had the kind of problem the janitors could fix, rather than one requiring the best of the best, or the "A Team" as the resident neurologist called them.

So dear friends and family, that's where we are and how we got there. I'll keep you posted. In the meantime, if you wish to serve us, please do these three things:

Pray. Pray for Alice. She is oblivious to what's going on, but what's going on marches forward nonetheless. We are begging God all the time to let us keep our little girl. Please ask Him that for us too. But we pray that God's will be done, and we cling to this promise: *I consider that the sufferings of this present time are not worthy to be compared to the glory that is to be revealed to us.* The future, barring an unusual Providential intervention, seems bleak. But who knows, God is God, and does as He pleases. May He please to be merciful to Alice, and to us, that we not have sorrow upon sorrow.

Pray for our other five children. These are perilous days for their souls. I'd far rather lose Alice for a few short years than lose one of my children for eternity because they turned their back on God, feeling that He's turned His back on them. God save all my kids – now, but especially forever.

Cry. God is in this, and we are absolutely stunned at the tears shed in God's presence for our little Alice. The tears of the men of God in particular are jewels adorning Alice's life. If tears are stored in God's bottle, it would seem he has a barrel full for those shed for Alice, and they are indeed precious. As one of the elders of our church stood in our driveway with tears streaming down his face, I thanked God to be surrounded by godly men with soft hearts. We know in this age of information there's a zillion different cures for cancer, and the time will come for you to share those with us. But for now, we just need to cry and seek God's face with you, and the time for those conversations will come later.

Comfort: We love hearing from our friends and family, and if you like, leave a note here on this page. We need you. We hope you understand that we can't physically or emotionally respond to everyone, but your kind words and deeds do not go unnoticed. They minister much grace and peace to our hearts.

There is much more to say, and I'm sure I could have said what I did say in a better, more gracious way. But thank you for entering this trial with us. To the dear folks at Quamba who haven't fully let us go yet, and the beloved saints at Lewis Lake who have embraced us as one of their own already[2], to our family and our friends, and to those of you

---

[2] On Sept. 1 I began my first ever position in full-time vocational pastoral ministry at Lewis Lake Covenant Church, which meant leaving the dear people at Quamba Baptist Church, who had loved us so well for the two and a half years we were with them. Since Lewis Lake and Quamba are each about 25-30 minute drives from our

we've never met but God has called you to our side to bear this burden with us, we are so grateful.

God help us.

joe and shelly, natalie, joe, emily, kylie, alice, and violet.

---

house (and each other) we were able to remain in our house and in the same community, so it's like having two church families.

photo credit Miranda Reed

This picture hangs on the wall of my office.
Alice on her fourth birthday, just home from the hospital.

Chapter 2

Biopsy Day

September 29, 2017

First, Shelly and I have been absolutely overwhelmed by the outpouring of love and support we have received the last couple of days. As I write that, it sounds so cliché, so let me try again. The bride of Christ, often belittled and maligned for her dysfunction, has dazzled us with her tenderness, compassion, and affection. Jesus doesn't marry down, and although His work with His bride isn't done yet, we've been privileged to see something of what He sees in her, and I have to tell you, it's awesome.

Let me catch you up...

Sunday morning we woke up in the hospital to find the nurses had put a "Happy Birthday" banner on Alice's door. They've been amazing in so many kind and thoughtful ways. The chief pediatric brain tumor doctor[3] thought since it would take a couple days to assemble a team to do the biopsy, and Alice was stable, we should take her home so she could celebrate her birthday. So on Sunday evening we packed up, squashed all eight of us in our seven passenger van, and headed home. We had no sooner gotten on the road than Alice's voice came from the

---

[3] "Oncologist" would be the proper term, but I didn't know what that word meant when I wrote this. Besides, as you'll discover, I had (and still do to some degree) an aversion to using technical medical terminology that I didn't understand too well. In a day when everybody is a medical expert thanks to the internet, I don't mind revealing my ignorance a bit.

back seat singing a SpongeBob song, "It's the best day ever!" It's hard to drive when you're crying.

Monday (Sept. 25) was Alice's fourth birthday. What a bittersweet day that was. I always take the kids just down the road to the Rock Creek Cafe for breakfast on their birthday. I barely managed to hold it together as I wondered if this would be the last one I'd ever have with Alice. I gave her all my bacon when she wasn't looking (She loves bacon!). She held one up, "Want one Dad?" That's Alice. She just knows how to do it. And she can eat pancakes, my word. A thick, plate-sized pancake, and she ate most of it, with three strips of bacon and a cup of apple juice. That's my girl! Ate more than me that morning, that's for sure. I gagged down a couple eggs and some toast.

Many of our friends and family were eager to come and see us and Alice, so we opened the door of the house, told them to make no appointments, just come. The last thing I felt like doing was scheduling visits. Screw it, just come when you're able and we'll figure it out.

Friends and relatives, hugs, and tears, tons of presents, and lots of prayer. When my Dad arrived at the house, I ran out to meet him like I was six years old again, buried myself in his arms and wept. It felt so good. Every one of the five pastors we invited came, from Apple Valley to Crosby, and prayed for us as our friends, as our brothers, and as God-called men of prayer. God bless these men for their service to us.

My wife stood like a marble pillar of strength, even through the tears. I've marveled at her these past couple of days as if we were dating again. I'm seeing a strength in her I've never seen before. I often say that I married her because she was so blonde and so beautiful, and later found out the incredible depth of her qualities as a wife, mother, friend, and child of God. Most people think I'm joking. I'll let them think that. I won the wife lottery. I had no idea what I was getting, and I got the best.

Tuesday we closed the door, and just spent the day as a family. Alice played "Minecraff" with her brother and sisters, and we took a trip to Chisago City to hang out around a hotel pool. Alice loves the water more than anything. But she was so tired. It was wonderful that she wanted to curl up in a towel and sit in my lap, but terrible that she didn't want to spend hour after hour in the water, like the Alice of two months ago would have done. Still, it was good to be a family.

Wednesday was more family, this time from Shelly's side. But it was tough. Alice seemed so weak. We cleared the house out at 5:00, sending home siblings, parents, and cousins. That was hard. Alice just didn't have much left in her. It was a really, really dark night. By Shelly's request (and I include that detail to my shame and her everlasting credit) we gathered as a family in our girls' bedroom and prayed together. How sweet to hear my kids storm the throne room of heaven on their sister's behalf. I prayed that we could trust that God loved Alice more than we did, even if He loved her differently than we would like. And they prayed similar prayers, in their own words.

Though we felt so utterly miserable, our misery has been tempered by the encouragement and prayers of God's people. We feel it, even in our darkest hour. We are stunned by the number of hearts stirred to pray for her. I say that to my shame too – I know something about desperate prayer now, and I see people desperately praying for my daughter. I know how incapable I usually feel to enter into other's sufferings with them, and I marvel at the ease with which others have entered into our sufferings. I have so much to learn, God help me.

That night our spirits sank so low. We'd seen Alice seemingly deteriorate before our eyes. Would we even have another week? Those were the thoughts. By this time though, we could hardly cry. How could we make it through the night? Before bed, I had to take a bath with Alice and give her a pre-surgery scrub-down. After hearing biopsy horror stories (and I wasn't going looking for them, either!), I wondered if I was preparing my child for the end. Sometimes the mind goes to incredibly dark places.

And then God's grace began to break in. We slept, and slept hard. All of us. We needed it, and thank God we got it.

Thursday morning dawned, and I got Alice's steroids ready. Four little pills, halved, smashed, and sprinkled on a spoonful of honey. As I walked over to the bed to wake her up, I remembered... Crap, they said she couldn't have honey, only juice. Waste not, want not I say. So I stirred in the honey into some warm water,[4] added some white grape juice, and gave it to her. She was sleeping so hard, she drank half of it, and fell asleep for 20 more minutes. I didn't have the heart to wake her up; Alice falling asleep in the middle of a cup of juice is akin to the Levite stopping for the wounded man on the Jericho road; it doesn't happen!

When she woke up and finished her medicated juice, the light was back in her eyes, at least a little. She played more Minecraff with her siblings while Shelly and I packed up. She laughed, she teased, she owned the room again. It was wonderful.

This will make us sound like something we're not, because sadly this isn't normal for us, but Shelly took to the piano and we sang *Behold Our God!* (for me) and *Jesus Loves Me* (for Alice). It was awesome. We felt a peace and a calm, on this of all days. We've taken to reciting Psalm 23 as a family, which we did, then crawled in the truck instead of the van so Alice could sit in the front between Shelly and me (yeah, it's probably illegal not to have her in her car seat, but screw it, we want to be as close to her as we can all the time. Judge me if you like, I don't mind), and away we went.

God bless Keith and Paul. My hard-working carpenter brothers arranged to leave their jobsite for a few moments and meet us just off the freeway on the way down and pray for us. They cried as the three of us, "the Reed boys," as we were once known, huddled together in a Park & Ride, and asked God for mercy. Alice gave them a hug from her perch on the front seat, and off to the hospital we went.

---

[4] In retrospect, what was I thinking? Is it no longer honey because it's mixed in with something else? Sometimes I marvel at my own brilliance.

The staff here (as I'm writing from the ICU) has been incredible. Alice's pediatric neurosurgeon spent at least a half hour, maybe longer, walking us through what he saw, what he wanted to do, and answered the questions I'd written out the night before. He is absolutely amazing.

It appeared to be God's providence that led us to the place we were, the doctors we have, and we felt a tremendous peace entrusting our little girl into their hands.[5] We had our questions, and some of them were hard, but they were answered so wonderfully well.

Our neurosurgeon showed us Alice's MRI, and talked about what he wanted to do. He explained the procedure so well, and made it sound as simple, routine, and safe as piercing her ear. One of the things we didn't anticipate was that he wanted to drain one of the "lakes" of fluid in her brain. One common way to do that is to run an overflow tube (this is my construction-worker interpretation talking, I'm not a brain-surgeon!) from the lake down into the abdomen somewhere. But his plan was to punch a new drain in the lake, a new outlet for a river (my words, not his) on the front side of her tumor, since the river coming out the back of the lake had been pretty much dammed up by the cancer. Amazing how God designs these organs. The new drain would find its way down into the same old riverbed "south" of the tumor, and her brain would figure that out and adjust accordingly.

Best case scenario, while he was in her brain draining the lake using a 2mm hose with a camera and some other stuff all squeezed into it (this procedure is called a third ventricular endoscopy), he'd try to take a short trip to the shore of the lake and grab a piece of the tumor, so he wouldn't have to do the regular biopsy. A traditional biopsy of a brain stem tumor is done by essentially running a blunt needle from the lower

---

[5] In part I wrote this in response to a number of comments to my original post that encouraged us to try different doctors, different hospitals, gather second opinions, and things of that nature. This was me saying as gently as I knew how, "We've heard you, and we're content right here." Over time, writing these posts became not only processing thoughts and sharing our story, but somewhat polemic in nature as well.

part of her head beneath the skull, if memory serves, straight through her brain into the tumor (for you carpenters, think of dulling a nail so it doesn't split the end of a board, and you get the idea).

Among the questions I asked him was simply, "If Alice was your daughter, knowing what you already know about her case, would you do this?" He looked at me and said, "Yes, yes I really would. This is going to help her." I felt he meant it, and Shelly and I both felt greatly at ease.

I also asked, "What do you think this is?" He said they were fairly sure, though not perfectly confident, that this was a DIPG type tumor. That's the nasty one, and the prognosis with it is quite grim. But they don't know for sure. Five days ago, not knowing what was going on was so frightening; today not knowing seemed somehow comforting.

I got dressed up in a big white suit, funny hat, mask, and booties for the walk to the operating room. I actually got to walk there twice. In a reminder of the futility of man's work, and the inescapable reality that something will go wrong no matter what we're doing, we marched straight into the OR instead of to the CT scan, where they were going to make a digital map of her head, couple it with the MRI, and use that to guide the scope into her head. The operating room perhaps the worst place to say "oops, we messed up!" but as we just arrived, it was the best time in the worst place, I guess. So out of the OR, down the hall (and I have to say, the hallways connecting the OR's are much scarier, more industrial looking, and much more businesslike than the rest of the hospital hallways!), into a tiny elevator with Alice in her bed, a *very* pregnant nurse pushing her, another attendant, and a random passenger. Claustrophobia, anyone?

I was so proud of my little girl as she bravely entered that giant donut-shaped CT machine. Somehow she managed to still recognize me while I was in my silly white suit and ugly blue hat (she called me "Baymax" from Big Hero 6), and still knew me even after I added a lead apron covered in Dalmatian stickers to my stunning attire. She hadn't been sedated and needed to hold her head perfectly still on her way in and out. I stood beside her and held her chin gently at the prescribed angle as her little bed began to move partway into that big scary machine. I recited Psalm 23 to her, and as I got to "Surely, goodness and mercy will follow me all the days of my life…" it was over. She was amazing.

Back to the OR. For real this time. I held her oxygen mask, first away from her face, then nearer and nearer (I'd get 5% of his pay, the anesthesiologist told me!) until her eyes rolled back, and she fell asleep.

I left the OR, went to a little room they gave me to change, took off my silly suit, knelt down, and prayed once again for Alice. But it wasn't desperate this time. Today was a peaceful day in our souls.

We even ate lunch. How remarkably odd that we wheel our little girl into a room, and while we eat lunch someone performs brain surgery on her. What a weird, amazing world we live in.

But we felt at peace. We could eat. We wanted to. Little graces.

Soon, the doctor came in with a big smile on his face. It went better than expected. He sat down with us, and said he'd been able to put a new drain in the lake, and it was a good one, it would work, and this would relieve some of her symptoms. We felt like, for a little while anyway, we might get our little girl back. I hadn't felt a thrill of happiness for a week. I have to say, it felt great. He said he took the camera to the edge of the lake, and there was the tumor. He got 6 samples. Tiny, but he got them. No need to do a regular biopsy. Another little grace.

He asked if we had any questions. I asked, "Can I give you a hug?" "Sure, we do hugs!" I hugged him and cried for joy. I think I hugged and cried too much, because I heard him quietly say, "okay…" so I let him go. But God bless that dear kind ridiculously skilled doctor, even if he doesn't like big long tearful hugs. I forgive him with all my heart. I wonder if insurance doesn't pay for hug time. Ha!

Alice woke up, asking for juice. So we gave her a cupful. And another. She wanted more. Whoa, hang on camel, let's see if this stays down. It did. So, more juice. And for good measure, one more; this time I watered it down. She didn't care. Down the hatch. That's my girl.

That's where we are tonight. It's been a good day. If we look beyond today, her future still looks mighty grim. And we're okay with that. Today God has proven Himself faithful, and the little mercies we received show us He still cares. One of those mercies is that Shelly and I are both absolutely enjoying today. We have today. Tomorrow has enough trouble of its own, but that'll care for itself. We got a win today. We'll take it. God be praised.

Thank you for your tears, and for your prayers. Your labors have not been in vain, in the Lord. If all goes well tonight (and they just took her off blood pressure meds, so they are going well tonight!), we get to go home tomorrow. We're so happy. It's a happiness we've not experienced before. It may be doomed to sorrow, but tonight we don't care. God has closed our eyes to the future, so we can't see it, but more importantly, we can't feel it. We are trusting Him with it, and we're good.

Chapter 3
Thoughts from Limbo-Land

October 3, 2017

At this point, we don't have much more to say as far as Alice's condition. Writing helps sort out the scattered thoughts of a beleaguered mind, so what follows is more therapy than journalism.

We're home, awaiting the pathology results to be followed by the process of working through treatment options. More thoughts on that a little later. I call it "limbo-land" because we're sort of in our old "normal," wondering what the new "normal" will be like when treatment starts. In the meantime, we talked with her doctor and reduced her steroids to half of what they were, and that's having some favorable results.

Alice effortlessly ate 4 boiled eggs for lunch today. To say she's been pretty hungry is like saying Spurgeon was pretty good preacher. She's been voracious. Hopefully the reduced steroids help curb some of that. Our biggest challenge is trying to help her not eat constantly, especially when everything in us wants to dote on her every wish.

Our church family has been incredible. Saturday night Natalie and Jojo went with me to a special prayer meeting the church was holding for Alice. They weren't expecting us, but we wanted to go and pray with them. We were blown away to find 30 people gathered together, tears in their eyes and deep affection in their hearts, passionately praying for Alice and our whole family. We recited Psalm 23 together, prayed together, and cried together. We are so deeply moved by the love these folks have for us, still relative strangers.

Sunday we packed all eight of us in our seven-passenger van once again to enjoy something of a "normal" Sunday morning. As an aside, I don't plan ahead well, even when I know mathematically that child #6 is going to mean we don't have a vehicle in which we can all (legally) fit. But my moderate disregard for following the letter of all safety guidelines opens up options that get us all squished in!

Mostly we went to church because we needed to worship. We needed to give thanks to God for His grace; we needed to express our dependence on His wisdom. We sang *"Remember Your promise, O God. Your grace is enough."* We needed that.

We were greeted with ribbons – almost everyone was wearing one – yellow with a gray stripe. Gray for brain cancer, yellow for pediatrics. We're so new to the church, I doubt I could pick Kim Swenson out of a police lineup, yet it was she who loved us enough to make 150-200 ribbons to minister to our hearts and remind the people to pray for Alice. God bless you dear sister!

Pastor Bob preached on "Be anxious for nothing, your Father knows what you need." It was awesome, and a great encouragement for our weary souls.

It's been good to be spending these last days with Alice, Shelly, and the family, unencumbered by the typical attention-grabbing, time-consuming tasks of normal life.

In times of upheaval and uncertainty, it seems our minds try to take the pieces that compose the puzzle of life and somehow figure out how they all fit together to make a bigger, more beautiful picture. We need to know that all the little pieces, especially the ugly ones, are both necessary and useful. And I have to say, there are some really big and ugly pieces we just found in our puzzle, and we are struggling to find how they could ever be part of something pretty. We didn't want these pieces. We still don't, to be honest. In the first days, we all said at various times we hoped we'd wake up and find it was all a dream.

But it's not a dream; it's not even a nightmare. This is happening, this is a part of our life. We believe the Great Puzzle-Designer knows how to make a beautiful puzzle even with really ugly pieces. After all, what is the cross of Christ but an ugly, yet necessary piece woven into the tapestry of the most beautiful story of all? If the execution of Jesus, attended by the sobs and tears of Mary, could result in such glory, might not a tumor in the brain of my little girl, attended by the tears of my beloved wife, somehow result in something so wonderful that we'll actually, meaningfully, sincerely say, "Thank you Father, for crafting such a beautiful puzzle out of the pieces of our life!"

The Apostle Paul wrestled through the reality of life in a world where things end badly for everyone – no one escapes the grave – and what's more, almost without exception, we don't reach the grave without a significant amount of trauma *en route*. Yet God says through his pen that "the sufferings of this present time are not worthy to be compared to the glory that is to be revealed."

If that's true, (and it is!) we'll be ok somehow. The challenge, of course, is actually *believing* it when I'm staring into the eyes of my little girl, feeling like she's got a bomb in her head exploding in slow motion. My head believes; my heart is sometimes slow to catch up. How can this kind of suffering that we're going through ever be worth it?

The answer that comes to mind so often is this: I don't know how it could ever be worth it! Anything *that* worthy is entirely beyond the realm of my experience. I've told a couple of people, "If losing Alice meant world peace, leave the world at war, and leave me Alice!" I can think of nothing that would make this "worth it." But I believe in a God who doesn't show all His cards, and who has surprises in store for Alice and for the rest of us that actually will make this ordeal, however it finally resolves itself, "not worthy to be compared" to the ultimate resolution. After all, isn't that the point of the phrase "the glory *to be revealed?*" It's not revealed yet. We don't know what the results of this suffering are. We must trust that when it is, we'll actually be jubilant about it.

But honestly, sometimes that seems far off. So we pray, God help us trust. We believe, help our unbelief! It's one thing to believe when it doesn't cost much in the way of emotional output; it's quite another to believe when we're trying desperately to accept the fact that this piece of our puzzle has to fit in somewhere.

We want truth. When the sun is shiny and the biggest problem we have in the Reed house is the fact that the eggs coming out of the coop are plastered with crap, cutesy coffee-cup phrases and bumper-sticker Christianity seem so charming. Chicken soup for the soul is fine, if your soul only has a minor cough.

We don't cling to the Bible as a crutch. God is our witness, we never did. We believe it because it's true, and if it wasn't, we'd drop it and go on to something else. I'm an optimist, and I hope for the best, but so help me, I've got no time for living in a dream world of make-believe. But we are now living in a world where hard truth is hard to come by. Our world is full of maybe, probably, might happen, should, most likely, and wait and see because we don't know. We're looking at a future that's incredibly foggy.

So we need something to grab on to that doesn't move. "God loves Alice more than we do," seems to be one of those helpful rocks on which we are anchoring our souls. He loves her unlike we would if we were Him, that's a fact, but that doesn't mean He must love her less.

This thing with Alice hurts. I like to think I have dragon scales covering most of my soul; not much hurts. But God is a sharpshooter, and he doesn't bounce arrows off the scales, He drives them into the heart, and they hurt. I used to sometimes imagine what it might be like to go through something like this, but it never hurt this bad. In my mind's eye, all the theology came rushing in, and I faced the fiercest of foes with a smile on my face and a song of victory on my lips.

Don't I think a lot of myself?

The theology is still there, and I need it, and it's holding strong. The song is still there, and I sing it, and my soul is moved. The comfort of brothers and sisters is there, and we are swimming in an ocean of affection we never knew existed.

But it still hurts. Bad. Deep. It hurts when I look at Alice and see the effects of this tumor on her face and in her body. It hurts when I look at my wife and see the pain in her heart. I like to be Mr. Fix-it for her. And I can't fix this one. I like to be Mr. Homeland Security, but this snuck in and I couldn't do a thing to stop it. The feeling of helplessness sucks.

God give us wisdom. We live in an age of information. But it turns out, not all available "information" agrees with itself. God help us to navigate our way through. One expert's cure is another expert's poison. Amazingly, according to the internet, none of them ever seem to fail! I've heard of so many successes, but only privately have we heard a couple of times, "we tried this for our daughter, but it didn't work, and we lost her." Strangely perhaps, those stories of "failure" are the most comforting. In the glamorized internet world where the successes are set before us, tantalizing us with promises of the weird being miraculous, and the miraculous being assured, the thought that we might be the only ones who totally screwed up and didn't do what we should have done, to the detriment of our little Alice, is really a heavy burden.

We find ourselves living in a day when it is more or less "common knowledge" that every problem has an avoidable cause and available cure, you just need to know what to avoid in the first place, and where to look in the second. The difficult downside to every solution that's proposed to us (and we can't try them all!) is that it leaves us with the feeling that if we choose the wrong one, we're ultimately to blame for the outcome. It's complicated further by the suggestion lurking just below the surface that if we'd only led the right lifestyle in the first place this never would have happened to begin with.

I've never been a fan of the Gospel of Nutrition, and even though justification by righteous eating alone (I believe the Latin is *sola non-deliciosa*) may soon find itself as a 6th pillar of the Reformation, I've never quite bought into it. Even though we face those moments when we wonder if there's something to the notion that we brought this calamity on our own heads by riotous living in the frozen pizza aisle or excessive revelry beneath the Golden Arches, the comfort I take is simply this: There is ultimately no hope of *anything* beginning or ending well outside the grace of God, and if God's grace is greater than my sin, it should be able to handle all our other challenges, which are minor by comparison.

Therefore, God give us grace. And as we say, God help Alice.

Alice & Violet

Chapter 4

Prognosis

October 11, 2017

I left our saga in "Limbo Land," the land of unknown between initial diagnosis and confirmation/prognosis. I'll pick it up there and catch you up…

Last Monday or Tuesday morning, Alice woke up particularly irritable and ornery. I wrapped her up in a blanket, then in my arms, and as we laid on the couch, I figured I'd try to make up a story to tell her. Lewis did that with Narnia, so how hard can it really be?

It's hard. I didn't get far, but managed to come up with a frog she named "Ribbit" who went fishing. Then she said, "Dad, I wanna go fishing."

"Dad, I wanna go fishing."

"Dad, I wanna go fishing."

This is how it goes. She gets something in her mind and it doesn't leave. She's not demanding, not entitled, just persistent. I knew my dear friend and brother in Christ Larry had a special place in his heart for both Alice and fishing, so I asked him if he would take us.

Actually, the way I asked was by taking a video of Alice saying "Please Mr. Larry can we go fishing?" and texting it to him. It wasn't at all fair; this was pure criminal emotional manipulation, and he didn't stand a chance. Of course he'd take us fishing. We set a time a couple days out, and Alice patiently waited.

In the meantime, we had good times and bad. On the one hand, we wanted to do fun stuff, on the other Alice was too tired to enjoy it and was pretty much done being "out." But one afternoon when we couldn't stand just sitting around anymore, Shelly wanted to go to a State Park, if nothing else it would break up the monotony. So we headed for Banning State Park up in Sandstone. Alice wasn't crazy about it at first and moped and griped for the first 15 or 20 minutes.

I wound up spending those first 15 minutes talking to someone from the neurology department answering questions about her recovery from the biopsy procedure. Pretty lousy start to our fun afternoon out.

But then it began to turn for the better. Alice perked up, my phone call ended, and the other kids started running and playing on the banks of the Kettle River, which was swollen and raging from four inches of rain the night before. It was really a sight to see. I tried, with limited success, to avoid thinking that a Job-like calamity was befalling our family these days and I was going to be watching one of the other kids swept downstream. Ah, how hard it is to just enjoy life, when it seems so incredibly fragile!

It was fun to see Alice watching the raging river and walk the trails a little bit. We enjoyed watching the other kids climb around doing stuff kids do – pitching rocks into the river, climbing around on slippery boulders and giving their mother heart failure, and all those things that need to happen at a state park. In the end, it's just good to be together.

On the way home, we picked up some steaks for the grill. We don't splurge like that often, but Alice in particular loves meat, so why not? It made for a good evening, and we enjoyed it greatly. Alice ate as much steak as we'd allow. This steroid-driven appetite is crazy. It's like there's no "full" on her tummy gauge. No matter how much she eats, she always wants more, and that's miserable for us, because we hate having to make her stop.

Next day was fishing day. Alice was so excited. Larry took us to Lewis Lake, where he'd done the arduous and sacrificial labor of "testing" the day before, just to make sure we'd catch fish.

Alice loved fishing. It was a day so perfect it couldn't have been ordered better off a menu board. The temperature was Laodicean, (neither hot nor cold) and the lake looked like a sheet of mirrored glass.

Alice sat in my lap, cranking in fish like crazy for an hour. The only time she isn't talking about food is when she's found something that captures all her attention. This was it. She smiled, laughed, and for a few blissful moments we forgot about the cancer.

After an hour, she wanted to rest. So I laid out a blanket on the back deck of the boat, set her on it, threw her own blanket on top of her, placed my sweatshirt under her head as a pillow, and she slept. Bittersweet, I guess. Sleeping kids are really adorable, and nobody understands the value of a good nap more than I, but there's also something unnatural about a four-year-old out to do what she loves to do but instead falling asleep because she's run out of gas so quickly.

I write all this, not to bore you with things that aren't particularly important or exciting, but to give you a sense of how we were feeling. Our Tuesday meeting to get biopsy results and prognosis was looming, and we tried not to think about it. We felt like it might be our last week of normalcy as we knew it, and we just wanted it to last forever.

On Sunday I told the dear folks at Lewis Lake Covenant Church that if Tuesday didn't arrive for 10,000 years, that'd be fine with me. I knew it had to come, and we held a sliver of hope that the news might be better than we expected. Still, since we really weren't expecting much in the way of positive, we were happy just to let it not come as long as possible.

But come it must, and come it did. Tuesday morning we got up early, spent a few minutes as a family reciting Psalm 23 and praying together, loaded up Alice and Violet, sent the older 4 up to my brother Paul's place (how nice to have a driving daughter!), and headed to Minneapolis.

Alice's appointment was at 9:45. We arrived at 9:30. As we got on the elevator, we were joined by a man and his son, about 11 years old, and a lady and her infant son, about Violet's age. They, like us, were heading to the 9th floor.

The ninth floor, we learned, is kid's cancer center. You don't go there if you don't have cancer.

As I said, we arrived 15 minutes early. In one of God's fascinating little twists of Providence, we sat in the waiting room for 45 minutes until we were seen. I think we needed those moments, because for 45 minutes we saw kids of all ages and all colors walk in and out of that place. We saw babies, toddlers, kids Alice's age, young teenagers, kids without hair, kids with masks, kids who could hardly see. I particularly noticed one sweet little girl of about 10 years old who looked really nervous and scared, but was doing her best to put on a brave face. The whole scene reminded me that as terrible as this is, it is a trial "common to man." It gave some perspective, and I needed it. God be merciful to these little ones!

We were called back, did the whole height/weight/vitals thing again for the zillionth time. Alice tolerates them.

Dr. Chris, the brain tumor specialist we'd met back on that first Sunday morning, Dr. G., who's been so good to us all throughout this process, and Dr. Tammie, who we'd never met before, all came in to see us. The moment had come; we couldn't put it off anymore. My heart pounds just recalling the moment.

Here's what we heard from Dr. Chris, in a nutshell, carefully putting my own words in his mouth…

"The biopsy confirmed that Alice as a DIPG tumor. (He explained the letters; it's Digressive something something Glioma. Google it if you like…)[6] It's a really crappy tumor. It's aggressive, and we just haven't found the key that unlocks it. It's intertwined with all the

---

[6] Actually it's called Diffuse Intrinsic Pontine Glioma. I leave my mistake uncorrected here because it reveals a frame of mind that didn't really care, at the time I wrote, to do a lot of research. I trusted the doctors implicitly and honestly felt that doing a ton of internet "research" on my own would only confuse me and make me second guess everything. To this day, I don't regret that decision, even though eventually we did seek a second opinion.

nerves in her brain stem, so we can't go in and take it out, which would be the best thing to do. But it's just not possible."

"We still treat these the same way we've treated them for over three decades: radiation. If we do nothing, she'll have two, maybe three months. If we do radiation, it'll shrink down, and Alice will have six, maybe eight months of good life. Then it will come back. That's all we can do."

What do you say?

Ah crap.

We expected something like this, but it still hurt. Hearing about likely time remaining, hearing him use phrases like "quality of life" and "palliative care" while we once again envisioned an empty seat at the table wrenches the soul.

Dr. Chris told about some clinical trials for this kind of tumor, explained what they were, and why they were closing – they just haven't been able to beat this one yet. Bless him for looking into them for us, nationwide.

I let slip the word "hopeless" somewhere in our conversation, since that is how it felt (and often still feels), and God bless Dr. Chris and Dr. Tammie for pointing upward and saying, "there's always hope." Every time I've turned to despair, the Lord has put someone in my face to draw my gaze upward.

It turns out Dr. Tammie has been following Alice's case through the hospital records, knowing we would be coming to her, but a friend of hers had also sent her my original blog along the way, not knowing Alice would be her patient. So how cool that even though we were meeting her for the first time, she's had an eye on us from the medical side and the personal side already. Dr. Chris said with a smile, "She's on all the prayer chains." We're so thankful for her, and again, for all the doctors and nurses who have been absolutely phenomenal to us.

We talked about radiation. Five days a week, sedating Alice, putting a custom-made mask over her head that holds it perfectly still, and blasting the crap out of this thing (not a technical medical term, you understand) with incredibly accurate beams of radiation, if I understand correctly, coming from multiple angles, all designed to hit the tumor and essentially nothing else. This buys us some time. That's where we are: redeeming the time. The days are indeed evil.

Dr. Chris walked us through understanding the difference between "what's best for Alice" and "what's best for us." When the tumor comes back, there are things we can do to eke some extra days out of her life, but they can make life very miserable for her. God help us, we want what's best for her, but no doubt it'll be hard to not give her what could prolong her life, even if it's just briefly postponing what seems, at this point, inevitable.

After they left, my wife said to me, "All night long, I kept waking up with the song *He Will Hold Me Fast* running through my head, and I thought, 'Why can't it be a different song??'" Indeed. Shelly says more in one sentence than I can say in a book.

We returned home via Famous Dave's to feed our always-famished daughter, tucked her in bed for a nap, and told the kids the news. That was tough. And yet, I don't know if it's because we've been expecting this kind of news, or because we're acclimating to this new reality, or we're just emotionally drained, or a combination of them all, but we don't cry so much anymore. We just don't have it in us. I feel bad about that sometimes, like I must have lost my soul somewhere along the way. But, it's just how it is.

This morning we returned to the hospital where Alice got another CT scan, this time to map her head for the special mask they're making, and they installed a little "port" just below her right shoulder. It's more or less a "quick-connect" for IV's and such. It's buried below her skin, and is connected to a main artery so they can just poke into it to administer the sedatives she'll need for getting radiated, and any other medications she might need to get intravenously. I guess if her life involves getting put to sleep at least twenty-five more times, this will be a help. But it's another procedure; another reminder of the difficult journey we're on.

She understands that she's going to the doctor but hasn't yet made the connection that she's sick. I'm glad – her innocence and ignorance are our bliss.

The remainder of this week is quiet for us. I get to preach on Sunday, and I'm very much looking forward to it. My assignment from Matthew 7:11 is "Your Father knows how to give good gifts to His children." No joke. Pastor Bob said I could trade it in for something different, but I think there's no greater text to wrestle through. If I can't look into the face of my little girl and know that all gifts from my Father are ultimately good, I don't think I have any right to stand in a pulpit and tell all my fellow sufferers (because we are neither the first, the last, nor the greatest of sufferers, by any means!) to lean heavy on God's goodness.

Speaking of leaning… We are still praying what we've prayed since the beginning – "Father, we wanna keep her. Really bad." I wrestle in my soul with how much weight I should put on God's healing hand. I'd stake my life and rest all my hopes on the truth that He is *able* to take this cup from Alice; I don't place quite so much weight on the hope that He *will* take it away.

I'm helped by three little phrases from the Bible – *who knows*? *if not*, and *nevertheless*.

David's son was dying, and he begged God to save his life. God sent the affliction, God could remove it. I take it that David placed all his weight on God's ability. Yet he said, "*who knows* whether or not God will be merciful?" I think that means he didn't lean too heavily on "God will fix this." Hope, yes. But a hope that, if not realized, didn't leave him tumbling to the floor, having nothing else to hold him up.

Shadrach and company were heading into the fiery furnace, and they told Nebuchadnezzar, "our God is able to deliver us. But even *if he does not...*" God is God, whether they walk into the furnace and have a leisurely chat with Jesus and walk out 10 minutes later, or if they are instantly incinerated.

"God is *able*" will hold all the weight you can put on it. "God *will*" can't bear that same weight.

Jesus was staring at the cross; His own horrifyingly brutal execution. He prayed, "If possible, take this cup from me, *nevertheless*, not as I will, but yours be done." Jesus could rest all the weight of the world on the Father's goodness, love, and ultimately His good purposes. But the hope that the cup actually would be removed, while perhaps giving some comfort, was never meant to bear that much weight.

Sometimes the hope "God will" isn't realized. Sometimes it collapses, and the one whose soul is resting only on that hope will fall with it. "God is able" is where we're living. We're still gingerly resting on the hope that "God is willing," but we're finding that we aren't placing as much weight on it as we did even a few days ago. We hope, we pray, and we believe beyond a shadow of a doubt that God is *able* to take this cup from us.

Will he? Who knows?

We hope.

One last thought: I keep thinking of the little line from Jonathan in 1 Samuel 14:6, "It may be that the Lord will work for us, for nothing can hinder the Lord from saving by many or by few." We're going to do the best we can to fight this thing with and for Alice, even though we can only fight with instruments that are, medically speaking, proven to ultimately fail. We are, by God's grace, prepared to accept losing her, whenever God may ordain that day.

Even though in my mind I've planned her funeral a thousand times over the last couple of weeks, I am constantly brought back to this: We still have her. She's sleeping in our bed, as I write. In an hour, I'll lay down my head beside her, she'll wake up a little bit, put her arms around my neck, I'll say, "You're so special, Alice," and she'll say, as she always does, "You're special, Daddy."

So we'll keep at it. We'll hope and pray and figure out our way through this, knowing that God is not hindered by saving with many or few. We'll do some things right, some things wrong, but we take heart that we serve and love and worship a God who can save no matter what.

We hope He does. And we pray with Moses, the man of God,

Make us glad for as many days as you have afflicted us. Psalm 90:15a

God help us.

Chapter 5

Radiation Week 1

*W*ell it's Friday night, and we made it through the first week of radiation.

And there was much rejoicing. *yay*

Following the biopsy results last week we tried to enjoy a couple hospital-free days as we geared up for the first week of daily runs to Minneapolis.

Here's what "enjoy" means these days: It means trying to live with the mentality that Jesus talked about: *"Do not be anxious about tomorrow, tomorrow has enough trouble of its own."* "Live for today" seems like a cheap cliché describing those who make foolish choices based on short-term pleasure, ignoring (unable to see?) the resultant long-term pain. For us, "live for today" means we're learning that thinking about tomorrow is like strapping a cannon to the soul and throwing it off a ship. It just drags us down into a dark place.

I was so excited to get to preach Sunday. My text was "Your Father knows how to give good gifts to His children." I titled my sermon *"All God's Gifts are Good."* Sunday morning I awoke to find my emotions coming out from under a sedation of sorts. Most of the week I'd felt pretty numb. Not normal, either. Just numb. When I mentioned this numbness to Pastor Bob, he said, "Emotions just get tired and quit working sometimes. It's okay."

Almost 4 years ago, when Alice was just 3 months old, I bought a really nice Bible that was a good traveling size. Then I had each of my oldest 4 kids sign the front page, so I'd have their names in their handwriting. I was looking at that page Sunday morning, and since Alice is learning to write her name, I gave her a pen and asked her to write it below the others. She did, and as I looked at her name there on that page in her own unique letters, for the first time in a couple of days the tears started to come.

We got to church and sang, "*You give and take away, You give and take away, My heart will choose to say, Lord blessed be your name!*" Alice didn't want to stand as we sang, so I sat beside her with my arm around her, trying to sing, mostly crying, wondering if I would actually be able to get up and preach or if I'd just stand behind the pulpit and break out sobbing. What a time for the soul to wake up.

I preached the promises of God to myself; hopefully others were encouraged.

We're trying to help Alice stay active. She's very tired, and hates walking for any length of time unless there's a really good reason to be doing so. She does love opening cards, and since nearly every day's mail brings something with her name on it, that's become something of a motivation for her to walk with us up and down the driveway.

Radiation is pretty boring, from our side of things. Here's how our days go: Wake up time is about 5:00, and I mash up steroids and stir them into a cup of apple juice, wake up Alice and she drinks it down. No eating or drinking too close to sedation time, so we've gotta get that done first thing. Then Michele gets Violet ready, I help get Alice ready, and prepare a backpack with a thermos of milk (usually toss it in the freezer the night before), a little baggie of Cheerios, and a honey bear. Out the door by six for the one hour drive. Alice and Violet sleep in the backseat, Shelly and I get to visit a little bit, and the older 4 stay home and sleep.

We arrive at the University of Minnesota Children's Hospital most mornings about 7:00, go to a room in the sedation/imaging unit where the nurse takes vital signs, meet our anesthesiologist for the day, and load up the bed with a couple little machines to be used later. I crawl in Alice's bed and she sits in my lap.

I set the laptop on our legs, fire up SpongeBob (the folks at Lewis Lake will no doubt be happy to know the super-expensive laptop they bought me is being put to the noblest of uses: watching SpongeBob with Alice…), and away we go. We get wheeled out the door, down the hall, into an elevator, go down a floor, down another hallway, past the "control room," down a winding, slightly downhill hallway where we pull up to whatever that big ugly radiation machine is. We're wheeled beside the table, confirm names and birthdates, the two radiation guys are there getting things set up, the anesthesiologist and his/her helper are there doing final preparations for sedation, the nurse is doing her thing, and once in a while someone else will be there if needed to help Alice keep calm, although to be honest, SpongeBob does that about the best. Besides, Alice doesn't take to strangers too terribly fast. So I try to handle the calming thing in my own way. Anyway, it's a pretty busy place.

They hook up a syringe full of white fluid[7] to her "quick connect" (my other non-technical term is "dongle," this little tube dangling from her chest. One end taps into her port, the other end has a threaded connection to make tapping in simple. Probably everybody except me knows what this little gizmo is) and once I see the nurse start injecting it, I wrap my arms around my little girl, tell her I love her, that I'll see her soon, and that she's so special. Within about 5-10 seconds she's out. She's lifted off my lap, or sometimes I lift her up and hand her over, I gather up her blanket, her special panda sleeping mask she always wears, the computer, and sometimes a teddy bear that made along it for the ride, and I head back to her room to sit with Shelly and Violet and wait for Alice's return.

---

[7] Propofol, I found out later. One day the head of the radiation department said, "You know, this is the stuff that killed Michael Jackson." I guess it's best to take it from a doctor and not self-medicate.

It stinks when I think about the fact that as soon as she's set on the table, they put this horrible mesh mask over her face so she doesn't move (think a hockey goalie mask, for zombies, and you kind of have the idea), everybody bails out of the room, up the inclined hallway and hides out in another little room, leaving little Alice, just turned four, all alone while they blast away at this tumor with beams of radiation. I'm glad she's asleep for it.

About twenty minutes later, they wheel Alice's bed back into her room, the anesthesiologist gives me the thumbs up meaning everything went swimmingly, and within 5 minutes, Alice wakes up. Usually the first thing she does is claw at the oxygen tube in her nose until it's taken away, and almost immediately says, "I jis' want some Cheerio-Bear." Translation: Cheerios with honey. Her all-time favorite breakfast.

I've taken to bringing three bowls, one for Alice, one for me, and one for Shelly, and some extra Cheerios and milk so we all have breakfast together. It's actually kinda great, even though Cheerios were never my thing. But they taste pretty great when we eat them with Alice. And lots of honey.

After breakfast, it's one last set of vitals, unhook whatever is hooked up, and out the door. In and out is typically between 90 minutes to two hours. Somewhere about halfway home there's often an emergency potty-stop for Alice and a semi-emergency "need real-food-for-breakfast stop" for Shelly and me.

Yesterday was such a beautiful day we decided to make a run up to Duluth to hang out by the lake and pick rocks, get the other kids out of the house and get some fresh air. But Alice was really cranky, really tired, and we found ourselves in kind of a dark place: weary, disheartened and discouraged. It just felt like always winter, and never Christmas.

Duluth was kind of a failure. Alice used to love this sort of thing, but she just didn't have any energy. I carried her to the water's edge and set her on her feet, she threw two rocks into the lake, and laid down on a blanket for the next two hours. It was fun to be there with the other kids, and we got some good pictures as a family always does on the shores of Lake Superior, but it was hard to see our little Alice, typically the life of the party, hardly able to muster the energy to sit up. We drove home greatly discouraged. Nighttime is the worst.

Today after radiation we had an appointment with Dr. Tammie. We like her so much. She helped us know that when radiation is complete, we'll see the old Alice again, and that lifted our sagging spirits considerably. We talked a little bit about the menace this wretched tumor is, and it really is wretched. She let us talk through our questions, our concerns, and helped us think through the alternative treatments that are so often presented to us. She said, "I know all about them; I've researched all of them. Believe me, if there was any of them that actually worked, I'd be all over it."

We chatted with her about taking a trip somewhere warm, sandy, and desolate when radiation is complete. We're a hermit-like family – we like going places and doing things, so long as no one else is at that place or doing anything there. But I digress...

On the way home today, I texted my dear friend Larry to see if he would take Alice (and me, naturally!) fishing. He kindly obliged, and Alice had so much fun on the lake. She was still tired, and again slept for a bit on the boat (not an entirely un-Christlike thing to do!) but really had a smashing good time, and it brought so much joy to my heart to see a few little glimpses of that steal-your-heart-every-time personality shining all the way through the steroids, the sedation, the radiation, and the cancer that are all working with and against each other inside that little body. And yes, she caught some fish!

I haven't quite figured out how to think about this just yet, but the type of tumor Alice has, DIPG, is essentially lethal, essentially all the time. I say "essentially" because somehow it sounds less threatening than just saying it kills everyone who gets it, which is more accurate. And that sucks something terrible. The available treatments can knock the tumor down once, maybe twice, on rare occasions even more than that, but the treatments themselves are difficult to endure, and this tumor just won't stop coming back, and back with a vengeance. We're basically looking at one possible outcome, barring Divine intervention, and it's hard to think about.

But the other side is this: I guess we don't have to spend a lot of time wondering what's going to happen. We don't have to carry this great burden like, "Are we doing the right thing, medically?" There is no "right thing" for this, at least if "right thing" means eradicating it, because it just won't go away and stay gone. And in some sense, it's nice not to have to bear the weight of wondering if we do this, or don't do that, and don't get the results we want, are we going to feel guilty for making the wrong choice?

We don't have to be desperate. In a strange way, I'm thankful that DIPG doesn't leave room for desperation. If both wings fall off your plane, there's no sense spending your final moments frantically trying to manage a safe landing. Better to just enjoy the ride as best you can. More than that, though, I'm thankful to the Lord Jesus that there's nothing to be desperate about, anyway. Jesus Christ, in space and time, went into a grave as a dead man, and walked out of it as a live man, and told us He'd do the same thing for us someday. Alice gets in on that, so I'm good. I'm good, because she's good. Resurrection is a really good thing. I'll be needing it myself in the not-too-distant future. And I'm so glad the resurrection of Jesus actually happened.

I've never been in a position of much leverage with the Almighty; it's not like He's ever owed me a favor. But I did pray in those early days, "Father, you can take her, but I want one thing from you... I want to *feel* that I get her back." I *know* I will, but I really want to *feel* it. The historicity of Jesus' resurrection has done that for me. That singular event which bridged heaven and earth means more to me these past four weeks than it ever has.

I still pray for a miracle. We pray every day, "Father, we wanna keep her. Be merciful to us!" But we do get to keep her. So I also pray, "Lord, keep us. Keep me, my dear wife, and keep all my kids. Don't let us go. Don't bend us so far we break. Don't lose us, Father. Give us what we need to keep trusting in your goodness and your grace." After all, all the Father's gifts are good. We believe that. Jesus said they were good, and He ought to know. He's been given everything. And He said He'd share with us. He'll even share with Alice. Maybe especially with Alice. I'm happy about that.

We have four weeks of radiation to go, and they're going to be grueling. Alice has to go in and out of sedation 20 more times. I can hardly imagine. We're so looking forward to it being over. And we're hoping it delivers us what it promises. God knows best. We trust him to guide us, to care for us, and to deliver what He promises. And He promises all things will work together for good. So be it.

Chapter 6
Radiation Week 2

*T*en down. Something like 17 to go. Early mornings, lots of miles, SpongeBob, sedation, radiation, and Cheerios (with honey!). That's our routine. It's amazing how fast it starts to feel normal.

It's working. Alice's smiles, giggles, and sparkly eyes are once again rather common sights and sounds in our old house. And that's been wonderful.

But the joy is somehow tinged with sadness, too. This is how it goes with her kind of cancer. You knock it down, it comes back. You feel like you get your girl back, but in the back of your mind you can't help but think you have to lose her again, and that stinks.

I try not to live there. I'm trying so hard to live in today, and if I must look to the future, I want my gaze to skip from tomorrow until 10,000 years from now, when faith is sight, tears are gone, and death is fully and finally swallowed up by completed redemption. But sometimes I fail at that.

It's no more possible to write a compelling and intriguing account of this past week than it would be to paint an awe-inspiring masterpiece of the floor underneath our sofa. It was just pretty boring. About the most interesting thing was making Alice oatmeal for breakfast instead of Cheerios one morning.

I was a little concerned Monday when Alice didn't snap right out of sedation per usual. Instead of awake and eating in 5 minutes, she slept for 10, then 15 minutes, after that I watched for another 10 minutes as she slowly woke up, as if coming out of a dense fog. The next day I did a little bit of asking around and discovered they'd upped her sedation meds, which I kind of suspected since I typically watch them administer the first blast, and thought I saw an extra little bit go in.

I get it – they don't want her moving under radiation. And it's possible to build up a bit of a tolerance to the sedative. But after I discussed it with the anesthesiologist, Tuesday and Wednesday we went back to the original dosage, and she snapped out just like before.

Thursday was another slow wake-up day. So I chatted with the anesthesiologist again about dosage and such – not to be a jerk, I hope – but I really want her to have to take in as few meds as possible. I was very apologetic about raising my concerns. Building houses, I know the frustration of having my area of expertise second-guessed endlessly by those who really have no experience in my field, and I really wanted to follow the Golden Rule as best I could.

So as I said for the fifth time, "I'm really sorry, and I'm not trying to cause a fuss, I'm just trying to understand what's happening and why," our almost daily companion at the hospital, Amy, said, "No, you're advocating for your daughter, and that's a good thing."

I thought about that on my way home. Alice couldn't speak up for herself, or have a halfway intelligent conversation about her treatment. For that matter, I can't have a halfway intelligent conversation about it, because this is all way beyond me. But here I was, trying my best to work with those who were also trying their best to help her, and together we were going to do our best to give Alice the best care possible.

I was reminded of our heavenly Advocate, our sympathetic High Priest, who stands between the Father and us, constantly interceding on our behalf. Sometimes it feels like this journey is going to bury us. How are we ever going to make it through? I thought of the Lord Jesus, who lived where we live, who almost certainly stood by the bedside watching His earthly father die, then comforted his mother, picked up his tools, and went out to provide for His now fatherless family. The thought of *that* Lord Jesus, in the ear of the Father, making sure that my family and I wouldn't be completely and hopelessly buried in these wretched hours brought great comfort to our hearts. It's good to have an Advocate in High Places.

These days, almost everything seems burdensome somehow. We've discovered, though we haven't yet figured out why, that when we step out of the house without Alice to go do normal, ordinary stuff, we are drained very rapidly. Michele took the girls out for lunch earlier this week, and I took Jojo to Cambridge to get his driver's permit paperwork buttoned up, but these little excursions, mundane and enjoyable as they were, consumed what little energy we had left.

So we are thankful for the people of God, for friends, for family, and for complete strangers who have stepped in to take so many burdens off our shoulders. We occasionally buy a gallon of milk – otherwise, food, excellent in flavor and massive in quantity, shows up at our door daily. Our finances have been of no concern to us – I can't tell you how many people have sent money to us, so freely and generously. A friend, out of the blue, spent a day fixing our woeful driveway. A couple days later, the man who owned the company that delivered gravel to us learned that he'd been running loads to Alice's house, so he and his wife stopped by with a pile of food from their church and returned our money. Amazing.

The weird part is, and I hope I can make this come across right, I now fret about my inability to acknowledge and give thanks for everything that is coming our way. We have been gloriously inundated by the kindness of God's people, and I worry that they won't realize how much we appreciate it, because I know we're going to forget to say thank you to someone, forget to send a card, or neglect to somehow express our gratitude.

We know, of course, that no one gives us anything to get a thank-you. But it's a weird feeling I've not quite experienced before. I guess most relationships are sort of built on this give-and-take system that roughly equalizes itself, and for the last month, we've been continually given to and have nothing to give back.

It's even been hard to just open the door for people to come visit, and that's been difficult, because we really do want to have it open, *almost* as much as we want to be alone. We're feeling like we're becoming buried in an insurmountable pile of relational debt. And again, I know that's not the case, and no doubt everyone who has helped us so generously would tell me to not feel like I do, but still, it feels that way. So these are some of the strange things we're having to work through in our hearts and minds.

Another tremendously helpful thing I've learned this past month about God is this: I don't think I could count the number of times people have said to me, in all sincerity, "If there's *anything* we can do, please, just tell us!" I believe them; I've said the same thing to others when they're struggling. Here's my conclusion: God programmed us to be this way. He made us naturally sympathetic to the struggler. Shelly and I would do and spend anything for our Alice in these days, but most of you would too. And that tells me that God has put this in our hearts.

It occurred to me (and my Dad helped me understand this) that people are this way because the God who made them is this way. We are, after all, created in God's image. And God is the ultimate Helper of the struggler. I've learned much about our Creator by watching His people come running to our aid, and running to us with tears, with encouragement, and with anything and everything that could possibly help us. It's not at all unlike our God who gave His only Son. Why? Because we were struggling. *Lost* and *damned* would be better, more biblical terms, but the reality is, His heart reached out to us in our need.

Whenever someone is driven, as if by some unseen force deep in their soul, to reach out and help us, I think about how they are simply reflecting the tender love and compassion of their Creator. We need to know, in these days, that God still loves us. We need to feel that God cares about us. Sometimes, to be honest, it doesn't feel that way. But we are reminded that He does every time someone says to us, with teary eyes, "I just wish I could take it all away!" What a marvelous representation of a kind-hearted Creator, yearning to come to the aid of His desperate creatures. So we are indeed thankful, in so many ways, for the many kindnesses to us.

Chapter 7
Radiation Week 3

hree weeks of radiation down. Two and change to go. Every day felt like Friday. It's funny how every day has a certain "feel" to it. All the days felt like Friday. Not the good kind of Friday feeling either, where your work is about done and you get to start having fun. This was more like what Bilbo Baggins was talking about when he said, "I feel all thin, sort of stretched…like butter that has been scraped over too much bread."

All week it seemed that tomorrow must finally be Saturday or Sunday. Oy.

But… Alice is back. It's so grand. Active, happy, playful old Alice. Essentially all her symptoms are gone. Eyes are back in line, she doesn't teeter to the left when she walks, she's not afraid of the stairs, and her right hand is no longer trembling. Barring a miracle, it's only temporary, but we're enjoying the you-know-what out of it. As Pastor Ivan noted to me this week, we're working to jam an entire lifetime of love and family into a condensed window of time.

I took some of the generosity given to us and picked up a rather inexpensive, 25-yr old Yamaha four-wheeler this week. Yay craigslist! Alice loves it; I knew she would. We go tooling around the hayfield in front of and behind the house. This afternoon we piled seven of us on it… yes, seven. Alice, two sisters, three cousins, and me. Good clean fun. Tonight we went for a little ride in the dark while the snow was falling like crazy. I put some sunglasses on her since she sits in front of me and it's hard to see with all that snow flying in the face and eyes. It was awesome.

Four weeks ago, Alice started on 12mg of steroids per day. She's down to 1/2mg a day now. I can't tell you how happy we are about that. No more endless obsession over food. Her cheeks had grown so chubby she would return from radiation with the tracks of her mask imprinted on her face, it was getting so tight. They are beginning to shrink down, if ever so slowly.

She had been going under sedation without having to add an anti-nausea medication for the past couple of weeks. But today after we left the hospital and just before walking into another appointment, she vomited all over herself in the car. My wife, always on top of things and prepared for virtually any calamity, had a spare change of clothes for her; crisis averted. It was only Cheerios anyway. And yay for leather seats in the Jetta.

About two hours later, as we were rolling down the freeway, Alice said, "I'm gonna frow up!" Shelly asks, "Where's that bucket I had in the backseat in case she got sick?" I say, "Oooooh, that's why that was there. Ummm, sorry. I was cleaning out the car and…" Before I finished my confession, she'd grabbed a cereal bowl, Alice vomited into that, and crisis averted again. I guess on Monday we'll have to start using the extra meds with sedation. Bummer.

So far she hasn't needed a transfusion. We're happy about that too. But she's getting closer to needing one, and it looks to me like we won't be able to avoid it forever. Hemoglobin and platelets need to be at a certain level, and they have been safely above so far, but nudging downward this week. Bummer.

She has some hair beginning to fall out. We were warned it might happen, and it is. So far it's minor, but it's happening. There may be a band between her ears around the back of her head that loses hair, and that's no fun.

I need to mention how incredible the entire staff at the hospital has been. I'd use the word "professional," but that seems sterile. "Friendly" might not convey how talented they all are. We remarked this week that somehow they make us feel like we're the only ones there. Dr. Katie, Alice's radiation therapy doctor, wrote her cell phone number on her business card the first day we met her and said, "Call me anytime. 2AM, whatever, if you need me just call." Brad and Rob are now our friends down in the radiation room, and they are so great, day in and out. Brad is a homeschool dad, who, like me, devotes a percentage of his income to late library fees. It's good to have friends to share some of life's smaller sorrows with!

The nurses have been incredible too. Amy, Suzy, Grace, Laura, and La'anna are Alice's friends now, and they greet her every morning with a smile and a laugh, and somehow, even after fifteen trips down to be put to sleep and radiated, she doesn't at all mind going "to the Doctor's house," as she calls it. It's part of her day, and she seems to rather enjoy it. The whole nursing staff waves goodbye to her every day now. Amy wasn't our assigned nurse this morning, but she stopped in just to visit with Alice and say hi. She's wonderful. The anesthesiologists too have been amazingly kind, personable, and very gentle. Dave, Connie, Staci, Dr. Wendy and Dr. B., and the ever-smiling Dr. Elena and nurse Martha give the morning some joy.

As Alice and I are wheeled from our prep room down to the radiation room and she sits in my lap watching SpongeBob, (and once again laughing at it, as of this week!), if you were to watch closely you'd catch the doctors and nurses traveling along with us getting into the cartoons too. It's kind of our thing now, and makes the morning go by with at least some levity.[8]

---

[8] One morning, though I don't now remember quite when this was, Alice and I along with at least two nurses and a doctor were watching and laughing about SpongeBob as we entered an elevator. The door closed, then it opened and we exited and began heading down the hall before someone finally noticed that we were still on the same floor. We'd all been so engrossed in the cartoon and laughing at it with Alice that nobody remembered to press the button for the destination floor.

Shelly and I are hanging in there. We have our moments. I attended a family birthday party last weekend and spent the first hour just sitting on the floor by myself, unable to eat, surrounded by family that I love very much, but mostly wanting to be alone. Shelly has the same kind of moments. They come and go. Mercifully, if I'm down, she's up, and if she's down, I'm up.

We went on our first date in weeks on Thursday night. It wasn't easy to get out of the house, harder yet to leave Alice and Violet behind, but we needed and greatly enjoyed some time alone. I like to drive the truck when we go out together – bench seat, 'nuff said! Shelly so graciously sits in the middle, yay me! We tried the new Mexican restaurant behind Casey's in Cambridge. It was really good!

We talked and laughed, unburdened ourselves of other matters on our hearts besides cancer (oh how I wish the rest of life would just stop and let us deal with one crisis at a time!), and enjoyed each other's company immensely. When we went to leave, we unsuccessfully tried to pay our bill, because someone else, we don't know who, beat us to it. That's never happened to us before, and it was so cool! I don't understand it – typically when there's a somewhat over-weight middle-aged guy making googly eyes at a beautiful young-looking blonde, responsible people call the cops, not buy their dinner, but hey, we'll take it! Thanks so very much, whoever you are, you made our evening.

Someone very kindly gave us, among other things, some incredibly delicious New York Strip steaks. So this week when Alice said, "I wanna have sticks for supper!" we had "sticks!" She was tortured by having to spoil her perfect dinner with a few pieces of broccoli, and I think her protests against the stuff only endeared her to me all the more.

We've been the recipient of so much kindness, and we are so thankful. I think every teddy bear Alice has been given has had at least one turn going to the doctor's house. She loves her stuffed animals and toys.

I often say these days, "We've never wanted to be prayed for so badly in our lives." And it's very true. We are still working through the emotional challenges of trusting in the love and mercy of a God who could fix this just the way we want it, when we want it (now!), but hasn't yet, and maybe won't on this side of eternity. But trust Him we must, and as my dear Uncle Fred said, to my great comfort, "He will not abandon you now." And He hasn't. After all, to whom else can we turn? He has the words of eternal life.

As I sign off, I've mentioned before that we like to say Psalm 23 together as a family before bed. Alice memorized it months ago, but we think the tumor made her unable to remember it, and she's frustrated that she can't remember it, then gets rather irritated when we say it together and she isn't able to join in. So, we mostly just say it after she's gone to sleep; sometimes she pretends to sleep and just ignores us. That's hard. But Shelly just told me that she said the whole thing this evening, complete with the little actions we have! How fun. These are joyous days, and we love them, and are squeezing all the you-know-what we can out of them.

Alice & Emily. One of my favorite pictures ever.

Chapter 8
Radiation Week 4

So we do not lose heart.
Though our outer self is wasting away,
our inner self is being renewed day by day.
For this light momentary affliction is preparing for us
an eternal weight of glory beyond all comparison,
as we look not to the things that are seen
but to the things that are unseen.
For the things that are seen are transient,
but the things that are unseen are eternal.
– 2 Corinthians 4:16-18

November 11, 2017

*T*wenty down. To date, we've covered about 2,700 miles going back and forth to the hospital, held Alice twenty times as she takes that big deep breath that means she just fell asleep, picked her up and handed her over to the radiation therapy guys. Twenty times we've kissed her face as she wakes up, peeled off the three EKG stickers she hates, and eaten many, many bowls of Cheerios and a couple bottles of honey. We've made it through SpongeBob season 3 and are well into season 4.

Seven trips to go. Almost there.

One of the little mercies we've received is that so far Alice hasn't needed any transfusions. Radiation diminishes her hemoglobin, so it's not unusual to need a fresh injection of new blood along the way. We asked if there was anything we could do to help keep the numbers up and perhaps avoid the need for a transfusion. We're told there's not, because the radiation shuts the hemoglobin factories down. Actually I don't think the doctor used the term "hemoglobin factory," so the keen eye will have once again spotted my non-technical, construction-worker interpretation of medical terminology.

Funny aside semi-related… one night this week I dreamt I was a doctor, and while I couldn't help my patient with his medical problem, I was able to help him figure out how to build the deck he was struggling with.

Anyway, back to hemoglobin… Because of the radiation shutting down the "factory," the count sort of is what it is. You can feed raw materials (think certain hemoglobin boosting foods or vitamins) into those factories, but if they're not operating, they're not making any "product." So far she's been well inside safe-level territory. I'm watching the downward trend of her count, and it seems hopeful that we'll make it all the way without any "outside assistance," if you will. Yay.

Alice continues to improve. Once again she likes to play by herself, something she used to do often, for hours at a time. The other morning on the way to the hospital I wanted so badly to freeze time as she played in the backseat with her little dollies, her sweet little voice sounding like the most beautiful music in the world. She even spent a little time in the shop with me this week. That used to be one of her favorite things to do, and something that endeared her to me in a special way.

Her appetite is down, her weight is going down, and her mood is inexplicably cheerful. Her nurse told us today that kids going through what she's going through just aren't as happy as she is – ever. She really is happy, almost all the time. A little sleepy, but happy.

And she says Psalm 23 again. She still doesn't like to say it with all of us, but she says it by herself, and it's beautiful. [9]

She vomited again this morning. That appears to be something we'll have to live with for the next week and a half until this is over. I'd just given her some juice with her meds in it, she drank it and immediately threw it up – all over the bed. Kids puking in beds used to be irritating to me, but somehow it's not so much anymore. The first night we got home after our initial stay in the hospital, I was sleeping next to Alice and sometime during the night she wet the bed. I woke up to find the sheets and my clothes soaked in urine, which I suppose under normal circumstances would stir up, shall we say, a rather negative reaction in me. Instead, my instinctive first thought was, "I'm just glad she's here to pee the bed." Better to have a bed-wetting Alice than no Alice at all. It's all about perspective, I guess.

I managed to score another pillow case today. When the radiation guys lay her back on her bed, they put a pillow case underneath her. Sometimes when we're getting ready to leave the hospital, when I scoop her up out of bed I unwittingly snag that pillowcase along with her. Of course, I never realize it until it's too late and we're in the parking ramp somewhere. Ah well, just put it on the tab.

Wednesday after radiation we made it to within a quarter of a mile of the house, only to come upon stopped traffic. As we got closer, we started to see flashing lights. Lots of them. Ahead of them, even closer to and almost in front of our house, a helicopter was sitting in the middle of the highway. *"Oh please, not the kids!"* A quick, almost panicked phone call told us our kids were safe, and utterly oblivious to what was happening in front of the house.

---

[9] One evening when putting her to bed, she recited Psalm 23 for me and I captured a recording of it. I posted it online and it can be heard at www.commonslaves.com/2017/11/17/alice-radiation-week-5/

We found out later a lady in her early 40's in a smaller car drifted across the centerline on the curve and met a Dodge Ram head on. She didn't make it.

I couldn't help but think once again how fragile life is, how suddenly it can change, how quickly it can end, and how many people find themselves in the midst of terrific tragedy. There we sat with little Alice in the rearview mirror and in front of us a scene of sudden, unexpected death.

Then I felt bad for saying, "Not my kids!" because *someone* was experiencing a great tragedy that day. This was *someone's* daughter, *someone's* wife, *someone's* mother. Maybe *I* wasn't personally feeling the gut-wrenching sorrow stemming from that accident, but someone was. And like never before, I felt really sad about that.

The world has lost some of its charming innocence over the last month and a half. I hope I don't go totally cynical, and I don't want to lose my enjoyment over the pleasantries still available to us, but to be honest, this world is just not as thrilling anymore. It's a difficult place to live; indeed, it's difficult just to remain alive – so many things can go so wrong, as we are experiencing. I'm just now beginning to be able to lift my eyes up from our own significant struggles and sorrows and see how much company we have in these dark valleys.

I think sometimes of little girls or little boys who don't have terminal cancer, but they're sex slaves, or I think of people who live in loveless, miserable marriages for decades. I think of parents who have to watch as their kids grow up, violently rebel, and self-destruct. What Shelly and I and the kids are going through is real, and it's painful, but it's by no means the only miserable thing going. I'm more alert to that now.

My mind turns to the Lord Jesus. It goes there because everything in me screams, "Someone needs to fix this mess!" This world is a stinking mess. Part of me, a big part of me these days, can't wait to get out of it. But more than that, I just want to see it get fixed fully and finally, once and for all. I want to live in a world where little girls live forever, where happily ever after really happens, where mommies never die in car crashes on their way home, where all the injustices are made right, the dead come back to life, and things are ordered in a perfect, permanent way, the way that I know, deep in my heart, they were meant to be in the first place.

Jesus is, after all, the only hope we have for that kind of restoration. The Christmas season is fast approaching to remind us of that once again, and I for one need the reminder. I'm learning, in a fresh and new way, to seek first His kingdom and His righteousness, and let Him add, and even take away, all the other stuff as He sees fit, until He's ready to finish the job He started back in Bethlehem.

Even so, come Lord Jesus. Until then, if You would please, leave Alice here with us. If not, we trust You. We'll just need lots of extra help to make it through.

Chapter 9

Radiation Week 5

If God is for us, who can be against us?

He who did not spare his own Son but gave him up for us all,

how will he not also with him graciously give us all things?

Romans 8:31-32

November 17, 2017

We're still figuring out what "*God is for us*" and "*graciously give us all things*" means and doesn't mean. Pretty clearly it doesn't mean God does what we want when we want it. But we're learning that it does mean when in the midst of the turmoil of soul, He gradually helps us know He inflicts no pain vindictively, that His love really does never fail, and that we can trust Him for the future, even if the future becomes that which we fear rather than that which we desire.

Twenty-five trips complete. The last full week of radiation is behind us. Two more trips next week, and we're done. I'm unsure how I feel about it just yet. Sure, the early mornings, smashing pills into powder, putting them into a cup juice, waking Alice up to drink it (which she hates more every day), driving sixty-seven weary but coffee-assisted miles to the hospital, lifting Alice's limp, unconscious body off my lap and handing her over to the radiation therapist, kneeling by her bedside as she wakes up, breakfast out of a backpack – I won't miss that much.

But I do very much enjoy the time I get to spend visiting with my dear wife as we make the journey, and there's something special even about our routine McMuffin on the way home. Soaking up Alice's smiles and songs emanating from the backseat – I'll definitely miss that.

I think of this tumor like a bomb exploding in her head. That's probably not medically precise, but that's how I think of it. Radiation kind of puts the explosion in reverse motion, and things are getting better. Stopping radiation means the bomb is going to start exploding again. Not today, we hope, nor tomorrow, but in pretty much every case (again I hopefully leave the caveat "pretty much" as though it wasn't "always," though that would be far more accurate) her tumor, her bomb, keeps going off, no matter how often it gets stuffed back inside itself. It's just yucky.

So in that sense, the end of radiation marks, for my mind and heart anyway, a new chapter in our story. We did find out today that the lingering radiation molecules will continue working in her body for at least another month.

Then... then we wait. I don't think we'll just sit and wait, you understand, we'll be doing life as best we know how, and jamming as much into it as possible, but to be perfectly honest, it feels like it'll be waiting. Tick tock... when does this thing go off again?

But that's tomorrow's burden, and I shouldn't be trying to carry it today.

Due to a strange convergence of a couple events of the past week, we feared tomorrow's burden had already arrived.

Alice has recently been complaining that her eyes hurt. Sometimes she says they're itchy. Since she doesn't complain either loud or long, we thought perhaps with her major decrease in steroids, her allergies were coming back. Regardless, those little things now sort of stick in the back of our minds.

On Tuesday morning we arrived at Children's Hospital bright and early. I was tending to Alice, no doubt annoying the nurses by hooking up her blood pressure cuff and pulse sensor and whatever else I can do to justify hovering over her and keep myself occupied. Shelly was on the phone with her parents who were at the hospital up in Duluth, tending to her Grandmother, who had been admitted the day before with intense vomiting. Gramma's not doing well, they said. Doctors say she has at most week to live.

I took my daily journey with Alice down to radiation, and after she was put to sleep I returned to her regular room to visit with Shelly about running up to see Gramma. By the time Alice's treatment was complete and she was wheeled back in, we got another call. Gramma was already gone. She was 85 and got to live in her own home until the last. But she really was ready to go, and rather anxious for a substantial real estate upgrade, which she at last received.

The hospital staff was so kind to us as this was unfolding. Dr. Tammie shifted Alice's typical Tuesday post-radiation appointment to Wednesday so we could get on the road and head north to be with the family there.

Soon after Alice woke up and had a little something to eat and drink (which isn't much these days; her voracious appetite has completely reversed itself), we headed home, picked up the other four kids, piled in the van, and headed up to the Iron Range, a hundred thirty-five more miles due north.

We spent the afternoon and evening with family hanging out in Gramma's house, which despite being full of family, still seemed rather empty without her in her usual chair. We left around 7:00, plenty tired from a long strenuous day already, only to be greeted on the road by a dense fog. As I strained to see, wanting to hurry home to get some rest, having to cautiously make our way through the soup, feeling exhausted with little relief in sight, life seemed almost unbearable. And thinking about Gramma's funeral details made our thoughts almost unconsciously drift to… well, we were trying not to think about it, but as you might imagine we were anyway. It was a dark ride home, literally and metaphorically, physically and spiritually.

Like cauliflower icing on a spinach cake (that's gross, right?), while at Gramma's I'd been watching Alice play with her cousins and I thought I saw her eyes out of alignment again. I hoped I was just seeing things, so I said nothing. However, on the way home Shelly showed me a picture she'd taken earlier in the afternoon and said, "Look, her eyes are bad again."

Ah crap.

The eyes, after all, were the telltale sign that really alerted us to this mess in the first place.

We made it home, fog and all, and crashed into bed, but our hearts were heavy, and our minds were tired but restless. What's up with her eyes? Is this all coming crashing down again – and before radiation is even over? Can we take any more thoughts of death and tragedy right now? We'd talk to the doctor about it in the morning.

Five o'clock came all too quickly Wednesday morning. I stumbled through the morning routine of getting the "pack-pack" ready (Alice's name for the breakfast-bearing backpack), making a pot of coffee, and medicating Alice's morning cup of juice. I was rather hoping Shelly would stay home that morning and get some rest, but she wanted to be present for our chat with the doctor. After all, she said, "if it's bad news, I want to be there for it."

When I went down into the radiation room with Alice, I mentioned to the guys down there about her eyes, because I wanted to talk to Dr. Katie, our radiation therapy doctor, about it. She was on vacation. But the radiation techs Brad and Rob, the anesthesiologist, Alice's nurse and I all had a little conversation about it. After Alice fell asleep and I was walking back to the room with her nurse, she said to me, "I bet you'll see Dr. Chris today." Dr. Chris is the head of the brain tumor team, and we like him a lot, but we've only seen him twice – once the day after the MRI, and once when he gave us her prognosis post-biopsy. So we only see him when things are bad. Oh joy.

I got back to our room to wait for Alice's return. Shelly and I talked a bit, but we were pretty well exhausted in every sense of the word.

We'd have cried if we had any tears these days. She had a few, but not nearly as many as she felt like crying, I know.

And then, in a most extraordinary case of really bad timing and miscommunication, one of our daily companions there at the hospital, whose job it is to make families and patients have as pleasant an experience as possible, but isn't really involved in anything medical, walked in with a book entitled *I Miss You: A First Look at Death*. She asked if we'd talked to our kids about death yet? Before we could answer, she said "Of course you have." By this time she knew us pretty well since we visited almost every day, and was certain we were able to handle the difficult conversations. Still, she thought this book might be a helpful tool for us.

As she talked, Shelly and I didn't speak to each other. I don't think we even made eye contact, but both of us were thinking the same thing, "What in the world is this all about? Are we about to find out Alice's treatments have been a failure and she's going to die in the next couple of days? What does she know that we don't?"

As these thoughts were swirling around in our minds a million miles an hour, we stood beside Alice politely listening but internally struggling to process what we were hearing when she said, "I'm sure your kids miss Gramma a lot..."

Ooooh... she was talking about *Gramma* dying, not Alice. Well, that explains a lot. She'd heard the day before about Gramma's death, and wanted to offer any help she could. It really was cool that she cared so much about our family to offer help for a situation unrelated to Alice's condition, but we were confused and not a little frightened there for a minute!

After that got cleared up (without letting on that she'd just scared us half to death) things began to improve. Dr. Tammie came to take a look at Alice and talk about the symptoms that we'd been seeing and said essentially, "I'm not worried about the tumor. This is from swelling from the radiation. We'll bump her steroids back up and this will take care of it." Okay, we can handle that. In no time, the increased steroids did the trick.

The week wasn't all stress and death. When we arrived at church on Sunday, one of our friends came up and said, "My Dad is flying in today, and wanted to know if you wanted to take a ride." When I hear "flying in," I think in terms of TSA, extra costs for luggage, and little packages of peanuts. But in this case, her Dad is a pilot, and wanted to know if Alice wanted to take a ride in his Cessna.

We went for it. Jojo wanted to come along too, so he rode in the backseat and Alice sat on my lap up front. It was great. I wasn't sure how Alice would respond, but she loved every minute of it. We flew over our house, and Emily came out and gave us a huge wave. Alice loved that.

Someone came from Memorial Drive Bible Fellowship up in Askov to deliver an unbelievable load of food and a huge gift of money. We were almost dumbfounded... again. We can't believe the generosity of God's people – to *us*, of all people, and the least deserving of any kindness! It's like living in a totally different life these days, and we're still trying to figure out how to live it.

Sometimes it seems like we have a different Alice every week. They're little things we notice, but they are "things." Before radiation, and maybe for her first week of it, her drawings were of "houses," which consisted mostly of drawing connecting squares and lines. Then she went into a stage where she just colored large, monotone blobs. This week she's taken to doing coloring pages, using multiple colors, and makes some attempt to stay within the lines.

Things are different at the hospital too. When we started, she'd be asleep for 3-4 minutes after getting back to the room. Then it was more like 10 or 15 minutes. This morning she was awake and smiling when they brought her into the room! That was a first, and fun to see.

When she gets put to sleep before radiation and I see the meds being administered, I always give her a squeeze and whisper in her, "I love you, have a good nap, I'll see you soon!" Three times this week after my farewell she cheerfully asked, "Daddy?" and promptly fell asleep. Oh, how I wish I knew what she was going to ask! Brad, who is able to watch her face, said "She smiles so big when she does that!"

Speaking of Brad, today was his last day treating Alice. He's off next week. I'm pretty sure there was a tremor in his voice as he said to me, "My family and I are praying for you." We hugged there in front of the radiation machine, as Alice lie sleeping on the radiation table, and I thanked him for taking such good care of my little girl. He's been so great, so friendly, and we have fun visits together every morning. I'm going to miss him.

It now feels like we have friends at the hospital. Some of the nurses stop by Alice's room for no other reason than just to say hi. Martha is our favorite anesthesiology nurse, and whether or not she's assigned to Alice, she comes in to say hi and visit, usually still in her street clothes and finishing her morning cup of coffee. She's so great. Apparently there's a bit of a competition going to get assigned to care for Alice. She's won the hearts of the sedation unit. Not hard to believe, but still fun to hear. Amy told me today, "You guys have quite a fan club here." Somehow everywhere we turn, we're blessed with love and support.

We'd love to rest tomorrow, but we're off for Gramma's funeral after breakfast. We pray the gospel goes forth with power and clarity, for that would be Gramma Helmi's greatest joy and a most fitting tribute to a life well lived.

Chapter 10

Radiation Complete;

Giving Thanks

...the Spirit helps us in our weakness. For we do not know what to pray for as we ought, but the Spirit himself intercedes for us with groanings too deep for words. And he who searches hearts knows what is the mind of the Spirit, because the Spirit intercedes for the saints according to the will of God. And we know that for those who love God all things work together for good...
Romans 8:26-28

November 22, 2017

On the eve of this Thanksgiving, reflecting once again on that mental list of good things to be thankful for, perhaps it is best to say that this year we give thanks in faith, trusting the Lord we love that all things, especially the bad things, will indeed work together for good.

I'm tempted to give thanks for the things we like and hold them up against the things we don't like as little spots of peace in the middle of the storm. I'm thankful for skilled doctors, the ability to "buy some time" with Alice, I'm thankful for the support of family and friends, the outpouring of affection from the family of God, thankful for my sweet wife and dear children and the fact that they still smile and laugh in the face of the darkest days of our lives so far. I'm particularly thankful for every time Alice's little voice falls on my ear.

But I don't want to simply give thanks for the things that give me joy *now*. This year, more than ever, I want to be able to give thanks for the thing that I *hate* now but know will bring me joy *someday*. I'm thankful for a God who works cancer for good – for Alice, for me, for my family, and for everyone who has cried along with us on this rough road. So we give thanks in faith – "Lord, someday we will give you thanks for this, and really mean it!"

That doesn't mean we expect this trial will end how we want it to – growing old with *all* our kids healthy, wealthy, and wise. It *does* mean that no matter what happens in the next months or beyond, we expect this trial, like every other one we have and will endure, ends around the throne of our Good King, offering our heartfelt thanks for a love that gave us sorrow for a night, but endless joy for a perpetual, eternal morning.

My wife and I often ask each other one question: What do you think God is going to do with all the prayers offered up for Alice? We are amazed, encouraged, strengthened, and sometimes a little confused as to the sheer volume and weight of prayer lifted up for her, from all corners of the globe. I can only say one thing for certain – God Himself has moved His people to pray. To what end? That remains the mystery we are curious to see unfolded. Indeed, we don't know what to pray for, because we don't know all the options God has available to Him, and which one He's choosing to bless us with. We hope that all the tearful pleas for Alice's complete restoration are answered. Yet if she's not, still God has heard those prayers *He* inspired, and will not let them fall uselessly to the ground, will He? Surely not! So we are thankful that we love the God who works all things for good for Alice, and for us. We give thanks in faith, even in the face of what seems right now to be an ugly "sight."

Radiation is done. We arrived at the last day of radiation to find the entire sedation unit staff wearing panda masks in honor of Alice.[10] They even had a couple extra for Shelly and me. Alice only owns the original and best, an icon, a thing of legend, and even occasionally positive ID down in the radiation room. Alice's room, the hallways all the way to the radiation room, and even the walls of the radiation room itself were plastered with SpongeBob signs just for her. We can't say enough about how amazing the medical staff all were. To the last day, Alice never once complained about having to go "to da Doctor's house."

An MRI is set for December 19th and we'll see what the monster looks like after 27 blasts against it. In the meantime, time marches on. We're finding our new(est) normal, but don't know what that is or how to live it yet. We're happy, we're sad, we're relieved, and we're anxious. But as best we know how to be, we're thankful, in faith that someday we really will be thankful for the briefly unspeakably bad things that were worked together for our eternally unfathomable good.

---

[10] Pastor Ivan Fiske had given Alice a panda bear sleeping mask as a bit of a gag gift, but she loved it and couldn't/wouldn't sleep without it. Since radiation was early in the morning and she slept in the car on the way, she arrived at the hospital wearing it nearly every day. The line about "positive ID" refers to showing up in the radiation room and the technicians identifying her, not by her wristband, but by her panda mask, which was also on her photo ID down there.

Sisters in the Snow

Chapter 11
Life Beyond Radiation

For God alone, O my soul, wait in silence,
for my hope is from him.
He only is my rock and my salvation,
my fortress; I shall not be shaken.
On God rests my salvation and my glory;
my mighty rock, my refuge is God.
Trust in him at all times, O people;
pour out your heart before him;
God is a refuge for us.
Psalm 62:5-8

December 12, 2017

Three weeks since the last trip to Children's Hospital for radiation, two and a half months since diagnosis. Time is marching on, and sometimes it seems to be flying by at a cruelly rapid pace.

We have been feeling things we've never felt, thinking thoughts we've never had to think. The latest relates to this business of time flying by.

We pray for Alice's complete restoration. As do so many of God's people. We do not lose hope.

But we also know, of all the families who have prayed for their own child smitten with this particularly wretched tumor, in essentially every case, God has provided neither medical nor miraculous healing. As St. Jude's, the best in the world at this point, says concerning DIPG, "there is currently no cure…"

We try to walk that balance between living with hope in what could happen by God's grace and living with the grim reality of what always happens with this kind of disease. There's no sense pretending to know the future; at the same time there's no sense pretending that without a doubt we will be the exception to the "rule."

So back to time flying by... One of the unforeseen difficulties we've found is the pressure to make every moment count; to make every event memorable – and meticulously record it. The burden to enjoy life is like a dead weight that just gets heavier all the time. To use a different metaphor, it's like staring down the barrel of a gun, watching an unstoppable finger slowly squeezing the trigger, and telling yourself, "Hurry up and make life count!"

The opportunities to enjoy many of life's highlights are plentiful for us right now; the pressure to savor how special the moments are is actually quite burdensome. It's made all the more difficult for us because all of life has this shadow over it, so the dark things are a little darker, and the things that are normally so bright are somewhat dimmed, making the effort to enjoy these days more difficult, and tainting the best of experiences with a sense of urgency, which kind of poisons them somewhat.

Hopefully that evens out. But it can be a rough ride.

The last time I wrote was the night before Thanksgiving. I felt positive, hopeful, encouraged and strengthened by the promises of God. The day of Thanksgiving itself was the opposite. It was, for me anyway, one of the darkest days of this journey.

We spent the afternoon at my sister's place with a houseful of family, generally my favorite crowd, but that day I wanted to crawl in a hole. I slipped out to the van for an hour to be alone, and later while everyone gathered around the piano and sang, I hid out by myself in the backyard. It was a dark day. I didn't have tears to cry, and I didn't have any strength left. I didn't want to share Alice; I just wanted hold her and keep her all to myself and let the world go to hell. I probably sound like a six-year-old with a favorite toy... I felt about like that too.

Eventually I gave the word and we left, rather unceremoniously. I couldn't even say goodbye; I just put my head down and headed for the door. That's all the strength I had in me. It was terrible. I'd love a redo, and maybe I'd do better. Who knows? It just stunk. Thankfully I haven't had any days like that since.

That debacle (for me, that is) weighed on my mind as we prepared for Alice's benefit dinner last Saturday afternoon. I'd be the first one to say we can't be slaves of our emotions, but I'm also rather unable to hide how I feel. So when the day finally came, I was a little nervous as to how it would all go. We had a really crazy morning full of cleaning the house before my mom and two uncles arrived from Michigan, (there's nothing more soothing to the soul than that panicked kind of "company's coming and we want to trick them into thinking we're not pigs!" kind of cleaning) then went to pick out and cut down a Christmas tree, finally saying a quick prayer for help, and almost racing out the door.

The dinner started at 4:00. We arrived at 3:05, and as we looked at a myriad of cars in the parking lot, Shelly said to me, "Look at all these cars! There must be a sporting event going on." There wasn't. I believe something like 80 people volunteered to help put this together. We walked in the door and were completely blown away by what had all been set up. Rows and rows of really awesome stuff that people had donated, that had been made, baked, quilted, knitted, painted, you name it, it was there, and it was amazing.

Alice had been looking forward to "her party," as she called it, but I don't think I did a good enough job of preparing her for what that was going to look like. But that's probably because I had no idea what it was going to look like, either. The reality was that it was so big, and so well-orchestrated, that it really was beyond us; it was bigger than our family. This was a community event; this was family, friends, brothers and sisters in Christ, people who cared about us, about each other, and we just enjoyed it the same as everyone else. That made it awesome, and we had such a joyous time.

I previously told Shelly I'd try to stick by her for the night. After we walked in the door we were almost immediately separated and for the first few hours I only saw her a couple of times, for maybe a minute each. It was a whirlwind. One of the organizers kindly but firmly ordered us (at least twice, maybe more) to eat something, which we finally did about 7:30, and after four and a half hours of non-stop visiting, we really needed it. So at least we got to eat together. For a few minutes anyway.

There was no official count, but the kitchen served up about 675 plates of spaghetti. It was a wild night. We saw so many dear friends, many of whom traveled a lot of miles to get there, and the only frustration was not getting to talk to everyone, and only getting to talk to the ones we did for a few minutes. It was a four-hour whirlwind of basking in God's grace and the kindness of our friends and family. We can't believe how many came to show their love and support for little Alice.

She handled it really well. She'd fallen asleep on the way there, and now that she's more her "normal" self and off steroids (hallelujah!) she's back to being a bit touchy and extra shy for a half hour after waking up. She came to life just in time for her big surprise: a couple young ladies dressed up as Disney princesses came and made a special appearance just for her. I was afraid she might just scream and run, and I'm not sure that didn't cross her mind, and as she approached them I could see this internal battle of happiness and trepidation going on in her mind, but she did great, went to see them, and they were amazing.

After the princesses, Alice disappeared with her cousins to play games and such; that was pretty cool. Then she came back to me, I picked her up, and while I was visiting, she fell asleep in my arms. When her puppy-dog balloon animal fell out of her hand and hit the floor, I knew she was really out. She slept for about a half hour or so on my shoulder, it took her about another half hour to wake up again, then the smiles came out, and she was off once again. It was great.

We saw people from all over; from so many of the churches we've been privileged to visit and preach in over the past couple of years, old friends from way up north, dear friends from the Twin Cities, even family and friends from out of state. There were people whose faces I'd never seen, whose names I don't know, there were people there who don't know us, all coming together to give of themselves for our little Alice. Once again, we wished we could freeze time so we could better savor each moment!

Our Lewis Lake church family – how can we describe their active love to us without somehow tarnishing its beauty by the use of mere words? They have opened up and poured out their hearts and souls into this little girl they hardly know. It's just wild. We're so blessed to be a part of them. Our Quamba family showed their continued to love us, which is quite startling because they actually do know us a little bit, and finally managed to be rid of us! Indeed, our journey is well-attended by so many loving, affectionate souls, in some sense we're traveling this rough road "first class," and that's been an unexpected joy and comfort.

I'm still learning about all that went on and the labor that went into the dinner. When we got home, Shelly and I sat on the couch and watched some of the Facebook Live videos taken. We were blown away at all that was going on that we didn't get to see. The crafts – how incredibly talented some people are! The baked goods – cardiologists must have been grinning from ear to ear thinking about how much business they'll get from that one night alone! And the auction – 200+ really awesome things that were given for Alice's sake. The Ogilvie School gave free use of the facility, the cooks gave their time, the custodians of their labors as well. Amazing. It will go down as one of the momentous events of our lives and stands as a wonderfully fitting tribute to the Little Lady whom it honored so well.

How is Alice feeling? She's Alice. As much as she ever was. And that's awesome. She remains blissfully unaware of her condition, not so much because we're intentionally keeping it from her because we're not, but rather on account of her utter lack of any curiosity about it, the absence of any pain, and... she's barely four. She runs, plays, teases, laughs, hides from strange faces, all the things she should be doing. She opens cards, loves getting presents, and what makes me as a Dad so happy is that with all the attention given to her, she remains sweet-spirited, generous, undemanding and despite our best efforts, unspoiled. She's a really great kid.

One of the secret fears I harbor is that Alice will be known for her disease, not for who she is; that she'll be thought of with a sort of condescending sympathy rather than being loved for all the things that make her so endearing. I really want her to be thought of in terms of who she is, not what she might have been. I want people to sorrow not because of the tragedy of cancer, but because of the threat of losing something incredibly valuable to all of us. I don't know if that makes sense, but it's a recognition of how I've failed in thinking about other kids in similar cases. I saw the disease, not the child. Somehow tragedies like this have the ability to dehumanize their victims; it's sad to see a child suffer, but it's not like they're a *normal* child, so it's not like their loss will be *that* bad. Standing on this side of the river, sometimes I don't like the person I was on the other side. I guess that's part of the process, and painful as it is to see myself in that mirror, I'm glad to see more clearly.

The older four have made us so proud. They have handled this entire ordeal so incredibly well. They've watched their little sister become the focus of so much attention, but rather than turn inwardly in feelings of being left out, they've joined in caring for and doting on her as well. I can't tell you how impressed I am with all of them.

Next Tuesday is her MRI, the first real look at this thing since the ordeal started, so we'll see perhaps what our "cup of sorrows" looks like in medical terms, and I'll let you know. Beyond that, I'm not sure what else it will tell us. We continue to trust the Lord's wisdom, some moments better than others, hoping for a release from the futility we've all been subjected to most unwillingly, trying to keep close to the front of our minds what life might be like when the hand of God Himself wipes our tears for the last time.

Chapter 12

Post Radiation MRI

You formed my inward parts;
you knitted me together in my mother's womb.
I praise you, for I am fearfully and wonderfully made.
Wonderful are your works;
my soul knows it very well.
My frame was not hidden from you,
when I was being made in secret,
intricately woven in the depths of the earth.
Your eyes saw my unformed substance;
in your book were written, every one of them,
the days that were formed for me,
when as yet there was none of them.
– from Ps. 139

December 19, 2017

S o today we went to see the monster… and there was no monster to see.

We went down with some measure of fear and trepidation; the unknown always seems to be a heavier burden than the known. We knew good things have been happening as far as Alice's return to her old form, but we haven't forgotten that just a couple weeks ago it seemed her eyes were crossing again, so honestly how good could it be?

Plus, we've been told that if the tumor is gone, it can mean a quicker comeback. So what do you want to see? Talk about feeling conflicted. I'd love to see it gone. But if that means bad news in the long run, does that mean I'd love to see it there?

Michele and I prayed together several times in the hours leading up to this, not knowing exactly what we should pray for. It always seems more fulfilling to pray for something that you feel deep down like there's some chance you might get it – and that's little things, more often than not: a restful night, a peaceful heart, a bit of good news. We still pray, "Please, let us keep her. Please!" But we pray other things too. "Thy will be done" seems to be more and more frequent. Sometimes it feels like a defeatist way to pray, sometimes pious, and sometimes, thankfully, we really feel like we mean it.

Alice had said the night before, "I'm gonna go to the doctor's house and see my friends!" And she did. She entered the Sedation Unit a returning hero. The nurses all came to see her and love on her, to marvel at how big Violet has gotten, and wish us all a Merry Christmas. It was like "old times," at least if one considers our five-and-a-half weeks of radiation "the good old days."

But we were there more for business than pleasure. I took another ride in Alice's bed with her on my lap, SpongeBob playing on the laptop. A blast of the white stuff, and she fell asleep.

Forty minutes later they wheeled her bed back into her room, and this time it took her about a half hour to wake up, which she did, a bit cranky to boot. Ah well, no matter.

Dr. Chris, the brain tumor specialist extraordinaire who we only see on really important, usually bad-news kind of days (not his fault!) came in with a light step and a happy heart. "I'm impressed! For someone who's easily impressed, I'm still really, really impressed!"

Long and short, Alice's tumor is gone. He explained that aggressive tumors tend to respond particularly quickly to radiation. I guess their retreat is in proportion to their advance. He went on to explain this particular mutation in a certain protein in her brain's stem cells that open the door to tumor formation, or perhaps more precisely won't close the door that prevents a tumor from growing. Basically (and this is my interpretation once again – don't go to your garage and try brain surgery using me as a guide…) radiation made the tumor go away, but the door is still open for it to come back. The medical field is still trying to figure out how to shut this particular door; how to repair that mutation. But that's the explanation we got for why it always comes back.

I'm in awe of our Creator as I think about the complexity of our bodies, particularly our brains. The more I learn about them, the more it seems improbable that any of us are able to live at all! There are just billions of little tiny pieces that *have* to be working correctly, and if not… well, this kind of thing happens.

It was fun, though, to see pictures of her brain without cancer. Right now, besides this mutated gene and an "open door," Alice is perfect. There's no sign of a tumor (to my eyes, anyway); it's gone.

Dr. Chris put it this way: we knocked off the leaves and branches, but the roots are still there; it'll come back. But not today. And hopefully not for a long long time. We pray.

I learned something today, and I wish I'd learned it a while ago, but better late than never, I suppose. On our way home, sitting down to a lunch of barbecued goodness at Famous Dave's, I was feeling pretty subdued and sad, either unable or unwilling to savor the moment. My perceptive Michele said, "Sorry you're not really able to enjoy this."

I like keeping an even keel. I'm prone to emotional swings, don't get me wrong, but I hate them. And I guess somewhere along the way I figured that this ends on a pretty down note, so there's no sense getting up too high, lest the downward stroke fall too hard. And that meant I didn't feel at liberty to enjoy what really is good news for Alice, and for all of us. Maybe it does come back bad. But today it's gone.

As I talked with her about how I was feeling, she and I talked about enjoying – really truly enjoying – the little things, the joys of the moment, even if the moment may be all too fleeting. Yeah, there's this big ugly thing over our heads and we fear a dark future. But there's a lot of little things that are really truly wonderful, and we should enjoy this happy day.

Sunday night we went up to Duluth to see the lights of Bentleyville. There we walked through a dreamland of beautiful lights, happy Christmas music, and bustling crowds excited to soak in the wonder of the season. It's truly a festive atmosphere. And I was able to just enjoy the simple fact that God still gives good things for us to honestly, and dare I say, righteously enjoy. Maybe they're smaller than some of the big ugly bad ones, but they're still good.

So I'm processing these thoughts, even tonight. This was a good day. Perhaps this ordeal still ends lousy, I don't know. But dampening the joyful moments of today in some sort of effort to lessen the pain of tomorrow may not be quite as good a plan as I once thought. To be perfectly honest, I wasn't sure quite how to communicate to you this particular chapter of our story, and still don't. I love that the tumor is gone. But I don't want to give the impression that our sorrows are over, or that Alice is fixed because they're not and she's not. Why celebrate successfully inflating up a flat tire when it's still hissing? But dang it, the tumor is gone, so why not celebrate it, even if only for a season?

Shelly talked with me about how many good moments we've had of late, and there have been lots. And we've enjoyed them. But I wonder if I've really let myself enjoy them as I could and should. Paul's line *"sorrowing, yet always rejoicing"* has been rolling around in my head today. I'm still working on it.

Physically, neurologically, and cognitively, at this point, Alice is essentially 100%. Except for some little mutant protein doors that won't close, she's as healthy as any other little girl. And that's pretty awesome. I'm happy about it. Happier than I have been. Probably happier than I will be tomorrow, but that's part of the battle that rages in the soul. Sitting at lunch next to Alice, she grabbed my arm and gave it a big hug, then laid her head on my shoulder, just getting close to me. Those are good times. Not all times are good, but some are really, really good.

I was talking with Pastor Bob yesterday, and he reminded me that there's no going through a storm like this without getting knocked around, beat up, and scarred. There's no cheating the system, no path through that doesn't really and truly hurt deeply; indeed, the pain seems to be one of God's primary tools for doing whatever it is He's got in mind.

So, we're probably going to get beat up in this tempest of soul. Okay. But I'm really wanting to make a concerted effort to enjoy those high moments when our ship pauses for just a moment on top of one of those giant waves which are just high enough that if you stand up tall and look hard, off in the distance you can just catch a glimpse of the safety of our final destination. Yeah, the ship is going back down into the storm again, and we'll lose sight of the horizon and fear being overwhelmed. It's gonna get dark and dangerous. But by God's grace we'll rise up once again for another life-giving glimpse, and someday, we'll make harbor, and the storm will be no more.

Chapter 13

Doing Nothing

"Be still, and know that I am God.
I will be exalted among the nations,
I will be exalted in the earth!"
The LORD of hosts is with us;
the God of Jacob is our fortress. Selah
Psalm 46:10-11

January 27, 2018

A good mother says, "If you can't say anything nice, don't say anything at all." If I could tweak that for my own purposes to explain a six-week lapse in recording our journey, "If you can't write anything interesting, don't write at all."

I could see myself morphing into Captain Hook – desperately trying to stop the incessant march of time. If only clock-smashing were less symbolic and more effective! It's almost sickening sometimes to think we're already four months post-diagnosis and two months out of radiation. The heaviest burden we bear is the stewardship of days that seem so much more valuable than they did before.

Of course, all our days are numbered, and of course the number could be "up" for any of us at any time. In that sense, one day is just as valuable as the next. Still, when you realize that the number of someone you love, particularly a little child, is probably getting really small, that realization is attended by an inevitable sense of *urgency* to wring maximum value out of each day.

It's interesting to ponder what "maximum value" means. Typically, it seems like it has to be synonymous with "maximum pleasure." A good day is a fun day. Boring or unpleasant days often feel wasted and weigh heavy on our hearts when we kiss Alice goodnight, another day gone forever.

We've done some really fun things. We hosted Christmas dinners for both sides of the family. Hosting is extra work, but for me anyway, somehow there's a comfort sitting in our own house that I lose anywhere else. I can't explain it, but I feel it. But Christmas was good. Family, food, presents, you know, all that stuff. "Normal." Trying to take pictures out of a sense of the happiness of the moment, not out of an unsettling awareness that, quite probably, this is our only Christmas as a family of eight.

We decided that for Christmas, rather than buy the kids material things, we'd try to "buy" some memories. So instead of dolls and DVD's, in early January we took them downhill skiing, accompanied by their aunts, uncles, and cousins. It was beautiful weather, good company, great snow, and lots of fun.

But we're learning something... I got Alice all dressed up and put skis on those little feet and took her over to the bunny hill. I was excited; she wasn't so much. With a measure of difficulty, we made it to the top of the hill, where we stopped while I consoled and calmed her; she really didn't want to be out there, and complained about almost everything she could think of to get herself off the hill and back inside. Still, she did a great job going down the hill, her little skis exactly between mine as I hovered over her, keeping her firmly in my grasp. But when we got to the bottom, she made it quite clear she was done. One run.

And yet, she enjoyed some wonderfully happy hours that day sitting in the lodge with her cousins playing before a window sill filled with their little toys, making fart jokes (I blame her cousins for teaching her those!) and doing what little girls do. It wasn't the fun I'd planned for her, but she had a great day, nonetheless.

In mid-January the Make-A-Wish Foundation sent us to a beautiful little house on the northern end of Anna Maria Island, about an hour's drive south of Tampa, Florida. Alice loves sand, water, and shells.

Michele's cousin Megan has worked in the pediatric medical field for some time, and she had begun filling paperwork out for us back in October, so for our part, the only thing we had to do was go to one brief meeting at the Make-A-Wish office in Minneapolis (if you recall during radiation Alice threw up in the car just before we walked into a meeting… this was the meeting), signed a couple things, and showed up at the airport.

I won't bore you with the details of our trip. We took a boat-ride, we found some shells, we hit some touristy shops, we came home. I can't say enough about how great Make-A-Wish is. They put together a really fantastic time for us.

While Alice loved all those things that led us to the beach, truth be told, she didn't seem to revel in them as much as we might have hoped. Maybe that's Alice, maybe that's us feeling the pressure to have the time of our life on the trip of hers, which is a pretty terrible pressure, actually. We had a pool in the backyard of our rented house down there, and she had fun swimming – once or twice. On the beach she dug in the sand and picked some shells. But to be perfectly honest, I was a little disappointed that she didn't seem to be having as much fun as I'd hoped.

The moment we returned home and before we even had a chance to unpack, she ran to her room and grabbed her giant stuffed SpongeBob and Patrick, gave SpongeBob to me, and for an hour I chased her as she ran from room to room talking, laughing, mimicking the voices of the various characters, and she and I lived in our own imaginary Bikini Bottom for a while. I almost hate to say it, but I think she enjoyed herself more that first hour back home than she did on the trip.

That's not to say the trip wasn't awesome, because it was. But it's a little window into who she is, and what we're learning about making our days count. Sometimes being home and doing nothing is the best thing in the world.

While we were away sunning ourselves on the beach, my two brothers and two of Michele's brothers, along with their kids, were at our house doing some pretty significant and horribly unpleasant remodeling. The idea was to change around our bedroom to a space that had enough room for an extra bed, should that ever become a necessity. They've spared me most of the horror stories of tearing this 115-year-old house apart, but I've done other sections before, and it's nasty.

How amazing to come home to a beautifully redone house. It's a project I wanted to do in the worst way, but between the challenges of disabling a major section of the house while eight people are living in it and my desire to enjoy Alice more than tackle a project like that, it just wasn't going to happen. They made it happen.

I'm learning that when God says, "My grace is sufficient," that doesn't only mean some inner peace or acceptance of the lot we've been given, it really means in a concrete way that God's people will show up carrying handfuls of His grace. A card, a gift, a hug, a sympathetic tear. A trip to Florida, a house more suited for the challenge. These are all graces that help us know we've not been abandoned by our Savior.

The day after New Year's we had another appointment with Dr. Chris. He had told us he would be looking into some drugs that may be helpful in keeping Alice's aberrant, tumor-producing proteins shut down, in effect helping to keep the tumor from coming back. So we were a little excited to see what he might have found, cautiously enjoying that glimmer of hope, and we had a couple treatment possibilities we'd run across that we wanted to ask him about.

The result of that appointment was basically, "We should just wait until the tumor comes back, enroll her in a clinical trial, and we'll go from there." All the things we asked about were met with some variation of, "I don't think we should," or "We've studied it, and it hasn't been shown to help." We left pretty crushed. We'd hoped there was *something* that we might do. But, nothing. Technically speaking, we've added Flintstone's vitamins to Alice's diet, if you want to count them as something. But that's it.

She's on no meds otherwise, and for reasons I won't take time to explain or defend here, her diet is basically what she loves – oatmeal, pizza, "stick," (steak) "crispus chicken" (chicken fingers), "eggs like a ball," (boiled eggs – she only eats the whites, "the yellows are for you Daddy"), "cheese circles" (quesadillas, but only the ones Shell makes, definitely NOT the ones from Taco Bell), and she's recently discovered what I've known for a long time – the joy of Dorito's. Oddly, after 3 years and innumerable boxes, Cheerios are off her menu. Won't touch them. So weird.

It's hard to do nothing. We trust our doctor; we have to trust someone, and he and his team are far more aware of both the problems and the solutions than we are. They're on top of it.

But still… it's hard to do nothing. It's hard because *nothing* seems like giving up, like we're resigning Alice to the mercy of a merciless disease. It seems like it would be better to do *something* than nothing. *Something* feels hopeful, it feels like you're fighting forward, courageously battling for the win. *Something* just feels more useful. Nothing is just dumb. Who does *nothing* when you could do *something*?

After three weeks of doing nothing, realizing how incredibly fast time is marching on, we decided to contact another pediatric oncologist at another children's hospital who has treated other DIPG kids, just to get her thoughts. Maybe she'd have a "something" for us to do.

We sat down with Dr. Ann on Thursday. She's a diminutive lady with gray hair, bright eyes and a friendly, intelligent smile. She reviewed Alice's most recent appointment reports, took a look at her MRI scans, and said "Tell me why you're here." I simply said, "It's hard to do nothing. We just want to ask you if there's something we can do."

Bless her. She spent a most leisurely hour and change with us, talking about DIPG, talking about clinical trials, talking about ongoing research, talking about things she's tried, others have tried, talking about the less-than-a-handful of patients she has had that have survived DIPG for over 5 years, talking about *somethings*, and talking about *nothings*.

I began to notice a theme as she was talking, saying things like, "Some families will do X because it gives them hope," or "If you want to feel like you're helping, you could try Y."

"Dr. Ann, I think what I hear you saying is that any *something* we do is more for our own benefit than Alice's, to help us feel better about helping instead of just waiting for this to run its course, is that right?"

That's about right.

Nothing has been shown to increase ultimate survival rates for DIPG patients; there's no real understanding of why those few who survived did. Proving causality is a difficult task. She said that of her three survivors, two did something, one did nothing. Others have done the "something," and it didn't work. Her best advice, formed after years of dealing with kids and families just like Alice: just make up your mind and do it, and you won't regret it.

"What if we do nothing?"

"You won't regret it."

That helps. I fear living in regret.

What's best for Alice? Every "something" has a side effect. It might as minor as her gagging on the awful taste of some pills we pulverized and mixed into her food (now that she's off steroids, she doesn't just inhale anything we stick in front of her!), it might be the side effect of traveling to a different city for a clinical trial and the discomfort of not being home. It might be rashes, it might be sore joints, who knows, but every *something* has a side effect.

The question I wrestle with is this: Maybe *something* makes *me* feel better, like we have some hope, like we're doing something. But statistically speaking, none of the *somethings* have proven to do *anything*. Say Alice has 8 months left, that's about the medical forecast. How do we want those months to look *for her*? She's currently playing in the kitchen with her dolls. I hear her little voice giving life to the imaginary world she's created as her dolls talk to one another. I see the joy she gets out of being home, doing nothing. And just about any "something" interrupts that at some level – with no certain benefit to her.

This has been our challenge from the beginning. Do we try to eke out as long a time as we can with her, despite what it costs her? We are of course, willing to pay almost any price; the weird thing is, we're also in a place where we have to decide what *she* has to pay. Or, do we make her days as good as we can, even if that means they may be shorter? To put it a different way, how many more days can we "buy," and what kind of days are they?

It's not that we haven't done "something." Radiation was "something." And it was costly – to her and to us – and it worked incredibly well, and the time "bought" has been and continues to be well worth the price paid. Dr. Ann said she's only seen one or two other cases where someone responded as well to radiation as Alice did.

I think of all the prayers offered up for Alice, and I once again thank God for His people, and for His grace to us, even in this trial.

But doing nothing is hard. It's not easy to do nothing well. But sometimes, it seems, nothing is the best thing. For us, anyway. For now. We wait, we hope, we pray. We try to live in the present in such a way that in the future we'll look back and have no regrets. But it's hard to do nothing and really believe we won't regret it. Then remember the main reason we're doing *nothing* is because it seems our *somethings* aren't ultimately very helpful. Thankfully there is One who is never doing nothing, always doing something, and sometimes puts us in a place where we can do nothing but wait for Him to do His something, whatever that is.

As I write, Alice is still "perfect." Other than some missing hair, it's impossible to look at her and know that maybe someday way sooner than I could have ever wanted, she'll truly be *Alice in Wonderland*, or my own pet name for her and maybe the title of a little piece I'll write sometime, *Alice in the Palace*.[11] But I still hope that's not for a long, long time. Until then, I'll be doing nothing, as well as I can, hoping and praying that the God who loves her more than I do, does something. After all, He has "somethings" that actually work all the time at His disposal. Still, by faith we know that even if we see Him do "nothing," there's still a greater, if now imperceptible, eternal "something" being done, for her, and for us.

---

[11] At this point, I had some ideas about writing a poem or a short story titled *Alice in the Palace*, describing as accurately as I know how, what entering heaven might have been like for her. I ended up using the title for something else, as you know, but someday perhaps what I had in mind at this point will materialize.

Chapter 14

Making Tracks

The Lord is good to those who wait for him,
to the soul who seeks him.
It is good that one should wait quietly
for the salvation of the Lord.
Lamentations 3:25-26

April 10, 2018

The other day the family was outside playing around in the snow – something we don't do often enough – and as Alice was traipsing about, I looked at her little footprints and thought, "Making tracks. That's what she is doing. Leaving an impression everywhere she goes, with everything she does, and if she is taken from us, her tracks will remain."

I suppose we're trying to, in some way, immortalize Alice by capturing as much of her as we are able so we can never really lose her. Every picture and video of her is, in some sense, one of her tracks. Beyond those visible things, all that she teaches us, or that God teaches us through her, all the ways her life and her struggle touches others around her are also her tracks, her mark on our hearts and the world.

I haven't written anything since the end of January. I suppose if we were living in a whirlwind of excitement and rapid, significant change, I would have. But it's been pretty boring around here. Perhaps the best way to proceed with our story is to frame it with some significant phrases that have come up along the way:

"We think you'll be happy when you come back in February."

Dr. Chris said this after Alice's first post-radiation MRI the week before Christmas. And he was right. Valentine's Day was her second MRI, and it showed not only no tumor, but it appeared to my carpenter's eye reading the MRI along with my interpretation of the Brain Specialist's notes in Alice's file that she had actually improved. Comparing MRI pictures from ones taken in December, I could see signs that she had actually healed some. Maybe the best way to describe it (and again, *totally* not a medically verified statement coming here...) was that some of the internal "bruising" where her tumor had been was clearing up. It's hard not to be pretty happy about that!

"When I finally gave up hope, I was able to live."

After my last post about "doing nothing," a beloved pastor friend from Colorado called me and told me this is what friend of his with an incurable, terminal disease once told him. The point: sometimes recognizing a thing is hopeless allows one to cease striving after the illusory cure and just get on with the business of living, even if it's only for a short time.

I'm amazed by the *hopefulness* of the human heart. Alice has, statistically speaking if you round down just a titch, a 0% chance of surviving this tumor.[12] Still, people often say to us, "Have you tried this?" or "What about this doctor?" or "You should check out this clinic" or "I know someone who did this thing, went to this place" or something similar. They are offering hope, and we want to reach out for it. We've

---

[12] As I've reviewed these reflections, I've noticed how often I say something like this. I did so for several reasons: First, to manage my own expectations by reminding myself of the near certainty of the outcome. I figured it would be way better to be shocked that she lived than that disappointed if she died. Second, it served as a justification for my decision to "do nothing." After all, who does nothing when their child has cancer? I suppose I feared being judged, and this was my defense. Third, in the days following radiation when Alice returned to "normal" and the temptation to conclude her troubles were over was particularly strong (after all, somehow it's easier to believe the one we love is the 0.01% who survives than one of the 99.99& who doesn't), I wanted friends and loved ones to remember the future still looked pretty bleak for her. I'm not sure those were noble goals, but at the time they seemed appropriate.

checked into this, that, and the other thing, we've hoped, only to come to one (pardon the ugly pun) dead end after another. Still, in our world of medical marvels and the audacity to believe that every problem has some solution, the hopeful solutions keep coming at us. Usually that's fine, and we try to handle them carefully, but all the same they often make our spirits rise in hope, and then after a little "checking into it," they fall, sometimes pretty hard. It's an endless battle to be appropriately hopeful, avoiding despair, but remaining realistic in the face of what this is: the deadliest form of pediatric cancer, as far as I know.

Still... the radiation did remove the tumor... so there's a hope that it won't come back... even though, according to the notes I read recently in a clinical trial concerning her kind of cancer, "recurrence is a virtual certainty." Nevertheless, I feel not unlike like that famous line from *Dumb and Dumber*, "So you're saying there's a chance?" *Virtual* certainty is something less than *absolute* certainty and leaves room for hope, yes?

We have hope because we believe in, are children of, and loved by the Creator of the universe. Still, I've yet to see convincing evidence that Christian kids with DIPG who get prayed for have a greater survival rate than Buddhist, Muslim, or atheist kids. Nevertheless, we pray in hope and are so grateful and still amazed by how much all of you pray for her and for us.

Lately I've been reminding myself that giving up hope that Alice will survive isn't necessarily despair that she'll die, it's taking the hopes I have for her – that she'll grow up to be as perfect and lovely and winsome as I know she will – and moving the "date of completion" back a bit. Maybe those dreams won't be realized for her just now. Shoot, for that matter *I* never grew up to be as perfect, lovely, and winsome as my parents (or wife) could have wished either. And in at least two of those categories, I'm trending the wrong direction. However, in God's good time and by His grace my little Alice and our entire family really will one day be perfect at last. So we always keep hope, somewhere. We only have a little for today, but a heckuva lot for tomorrow.

She's got enough problems, why does she have to deal with this?

Late February, spoken by my exasperated wife.

February was flu month in our house. A mild strain to be sure, but one that just kept going around and around, till some of the kids had one version or another at least three times. You know the drill – lie on the couch for a day or two, then make room for the next one. We all had it. Alice had gotten a flu shot, which this year boasted a whopping 10% effective rate. She numbered among the 90% and took her turns on the couch too.

We found ourselves trying to cope with the biggest problems we've ever had to deal with and getting run down by rather mundane little ones. By "cope" I mean "trying to have fun and make memories!" Instead, we sat at home and tended to the sick. Sick Mom, sick Alice, sick everybody. Being sick feels like a waste of time, and when time is particularly precious, we feel it more keenly when its wasted, that's for sure.

It's exhausting trying to capture every little thing!

It was late evening, when spirits typically sag, and Michele was going through the pictures in her camera.

It's really hard to live in "crisis" mode. The last four months Alice has been really quite normal. We sense this internal battle between the exhausting labor of trying to make each moment count, making sure to capture those special moments because who knows, we may never be able to have them again. On the other hand we just want to relax and put the weights of our minds aside for a while and live the rather boring life we've always enjoyed living, tucked away in our little old house, gathered around the table for supper, reading, watching a movie (she wanted to watch some episodes of The Three Stooges tonight, that's my girl!), or just horsing around till bed time.

Bulbous Bodies

We went to the Wisconsin Dells for a couple days with my brothers, sister, and their families. It was our way of saying thanks to them for remodeling half our house… in four days. Shortly after we arrived, I sat next to the lazy river with Alice cozied up on my lap. Imagine the scene –hundreds of middle-aged mid-westerners in bathing suits… in late February, all crowded just a little too tightly into an indoor park escaping the cold winter weather. As I held my little girl wondering about her future, I thought about my problems, and how hard life is. But looking at the cloth-deficient people all around us, I realized I was surrounded by more wrinkly, aging, misshapen, oversized, undersized, malfunctioning bodies than I ever really wanted to share a pool with. I was reminded in a new and strangely powerful way that life on this earth is just hard. With precious few exceptions perhaps, none of those people (and I include myself in that number!) were *physically* everything they ever dreamed they would be, and I know behind the outward appearance of almost every one of them was a host of far more significant, meaningful, and difficult relational, financial, and spiritual problems weighing them down.

Somehow in that moment I felt a strange kinship with humanity in general. Life on this earth seemed just plain disappointing, and Heaven felt particularly appealing to me in that moment.

Anyway, it was a great time spending a few days having fun in the waterpark with the kids. The sight of all twenty cousins laughing together as they went barreling down the corridors of our hotel was almost worth the trip. Still, Alice just likes being home the best.

Except Sundays. She loves going to church. We all do. A few months ago, Alice decided she wasn't going to sit with the family. Instead she wanted to sit with "Miss Cheryl," her Sunday School teacher, on the opposite side of the sanctuary, front row. So every Sunday, that's where she goes. She (mostly) quietly plays, colors, crawls in Cheryl's lap, and takes a nap. It's pretty awesome. Lately I've noticed that quite a few kids from her class are now sitting through the service with her and Cheryl, so she kind of started something. Cheryl's the best – she handles it all so well. Alice (and now her friends) probably abuse her good graces. But it's pretty special to watch anyway.

We want to be surrounded, and we want to be left alone

This is how I try to describe the multitude of mixed feelings we experience when people ask "How are you doing?" and want more than my typical "We're hanging in there." Every step of this journey is one we've never taken, and we are flooded with a host of conflicting, confusing emotions. As family, friends, and even some strangers have come closer to us to endure this trial by our side, we have found ourselves withdrawing more tightly into ourselves, creating distance between us and those who have been closest to us. It's the weirdest thing.

I've often thought in recent days, "What if this thing is back?" I'd want to open our house up and let the world come in and show off my Alice, because she's worthy to be seen and admired, in my incredibly biased opinion. At the same time I would want to shut the door and not let anybody in. And these paradoxical feelings replay themselves in a variety of ways in a host of different situations. I find myself feeling guilty for being home so much, for "producing" so little, so I commit myself to various projects, then kick myself for not being home. Still trying to figure that out!

If you see anything, let us know – Dr. Chris

We left the December MRI with the hopeful words, "We think you'll be happy when you come back in February." We left February with a little different sendoff until our April MRI: "If you see anything, let us know."

Ugh. They've seen this more than we have; they know the progression. It was really nice to not feel like we were going "see anything" for those first couple of months. It was nice not looking too closely, trying not to worry. But this time we felt, to some degree anyway, that we'd lost that freedom to relax.

The week leading up to Palm Sunday was particularly difficult for us. Alice hadn't eaten much all week, slept *a lot*, and complained of pain in her legs (probably steroids settling, we'd been told back in February) that became so severe one day she couldn't even walk until the afternoon, and even then hobbled around putting hardly any weight on it. That was also the week she stood at the top of the stairs and said, "I'm scared!" Ugh. Stairs were one of the things she lost her ability to do before.

Later that week she perked up some and went to an Easter Camp the church put on for the kids (which she loved!), and while she was doing crafts I peeked in her room and I swear her eyes were going crossed again. My blood about ran cold. That made for a really dark day, the end of a really dark week.

Michele and I sometimes play this cruel guessing game – is she not doing the stairs because she's spoiled and knows she'll get carried? Is the pain in her legs only remnants of her steroids? Is the weirdness I see in her eyes just me being paranoid? Are the late nights she sometimes has just exhausting her?

Or is it brain cancer?

We go back to Children's for an MRI next Tuesday. I guess then we'll find out. As we say, God help us. Truth be told, I'm not as optimistic as I was in February. But then, I may just be imagining things. See how this game works?

Anyway, God has helped us. He is helping us. His will be done. His plans are for good, not evil, and if they seem evil, I can hardly imagine the good He's going to work out of it. In this life, no doubt, but especially the next. After all, He's not safe, but He's good. Besides, at the end of the day I suppose we all could say that like Alice, we're 0%'ers. Maybe she beats us to the end, maybe not, but we all stop making tracks in this world some day and move on to the next. So God help us all.

Chapter 15
Puddle Boots

Now, I further saw, that betwixt them and the gate [of the Celestial City] was a river, but there was no bridge to go over: the river was very deep. ...The Pilgrims then, especially Christian, began to despond in their minds, and looked this way and that, but no way could be found by them by which they might escape the river. Then they asked the men if the waters were all of a depth. They said: No; yet they could not help them in that case; for, said they, you shall find it deeper or shallower as you believe in the King of the place.

They then addressed themselves to the water and, entering, Christian began to sink, and crying out to his good friend Hopeful, he said, I sink in deep waters; the billows go over my head, all his waves go over me! Then said the other, Be of good cheer, my brother, I feel the bottom, and it is good.

– Pilgrim's Progress

April 17, 2018

"*I* see two Georges!"

It was Thursday night, and Alice was watching Curious George. We'd been worried about her, as you know from my last writing, only seven short days ago. She spoke those words with an air of innocent amusement, as though it was funny, entirely unaware of what they meant for her. They may forever be burned in our memory as some of the most terrible we've heard in our lives. We weren't seeing things; her eyes weren't able to keep aligned anymore, and she was seeing double.

Friday night after Alice fell asleep we had a little family meeting to tell the kids what we were seeing and what we were almost certain was happening. We couldn't keep it from them, not that we'd want to, but we wanted to be the ones walking them through it, not waiting for them to figure it out on their own. Tough stuff.

Over the next four days, we saw daily changes, in all the wrong directions. It was basically a rapid return to where we were when this thing started. She's now rather wobbly on her feet, and often wears an eye patch Shelly made to relieve some of the strain on her eyes. It's incredible how much has changed in the last seven days. We didn't know what all the changes meant as far as her long-term condition, or for that matter exactly what was happening, so we publicly kept silent simply because we didn't know what to say. We had a pretty good guess, but we wanted to know for sure before we spoke. Shelly stayed home with Alice on Sunday; church is Alice's favorite, but she just wasn't in a place to be out and about.

As we thought about the MRI taking place this morning, our expectations were for nothing but a really, really bad day.

I like to read the Psalms on bad days. They help, because the best songs come out of really bad days. And I'm reading through the Psalms anyway. But the five or six I read this morning all had the same theme: "Things are bad, I'm getting creamed, then God shows up and comes through and it's all better." Except I didn't feel like this was gonna get better.

In the long run, of course, *all* tears will be wiped away. But I really want a win *now*. Sitting in her room while she off was getting her MRI, waiting for her return, I skipped ahead in my reading to Psalm 44. That's a good one for a day like this – no happy ending, just "God, we're getting plastered, and we don't feel like we deserve it. Please show up because you love us." (Joe Reed paraphrase) Somehow knowing someone else had been in my shoes before was helpful. Two months before Alice's diagnosis I preached a sermon from that Psalm, "*When*

God Takes the Wheels Off." Boy did He ever. I think of that Psalm often, and it scarcely fails to bring some comfort.

After the MRI, Dr. Chris and Tammy came in our room, this time without the usual entourage of scribes, interns, and others, and said basically, "What you suspected is happening. There is progression." No real shock there.

"Here's some options for you to consider..." (I'll keep those to myself for now, since we're still pondering them. Sadly the options we have really change nothing, just how it happens...)

"Doctor Chris, you've seen this more than we have, you sort of know how this goes, what can we expect?" The million-dollar question.

"With the rapid decline in her motor skills and the growth of the tumor, and knowing all things are in God's hands, you can probably expect a month to six more weeks."

Four to six weeks? I was prepared for bad news, but not that bad. Ah crap.

We cried. Tammy cried. When Alice's favorite nurse Amy came back in the room, she cried. We hugged each other, and Alice slept. And that's good. She's confused by Dad crying.

I titled this "Puddle Boots" because on the way home today I was thinking about that river crossing scene that Bunyan painted so vividly as he pictured death. For some, death was like crossing a raging, deep river. For others, it's like wading across a shallow stream. Our task, so far as God helps us, is over these next few weeks to try to make it so she can cross in her puddle boots. I'm not even sure quite how to do that, but that's my job now, and I'm going to do the best I can. And dear Jesus please, if she must cross, give her a shallow crossing.

Last week I had taken her on a whim to Walmart to get some snacks (and always a toy or two – I can't resist making her day), and on the way back, with heavy thoughts on my mind, as she sat next to me on the front seat of the truck, I said to her, "Alice, did you know your Daddy loves you?"

"Yes!"

"Alice, do you know Jesus loves you?"

"Yes!"

"Alice, pretty soon Jesus is going to send some of his friends to get you so you can go visit him, ok? They're really nice and you don't have to be afraid."

"Okay."

Then she looked up at me with a smile and a twinkle in her eye and said, "But you can't come with!"

Not yet. But soon enough.

I bought a trampoline for Alice that was delivered last week, just before the big snowstorm. While we were at the hospital today, the kids set it up. She loves it. Who knows how many days she'll be able to use it, but today she's able to at least bounce around, mostly on her knees.

Our plan right now is to be home as much as humanly possible. These are her days, so we will be arranging them accordingly. While we'd love to, as I wrote before, open the doors to any and all, the reality is that Alice is comfortable around precious few people. So we're planning a lot of peace and quiet, and we'll reach out to her favorite people to make sure she gets to see them.

Pray for us. These are hard days, as you can imagine. It's not like we didn't see them coming, and if anything, worked extra hard to keep ourselves cognizant of their impending arrival. But we didn't expect them to come so soon and hit with such ferocity, so it *still* feels like a kick in the gut.

We often find ourselves echoing the opening chapters of Job's complaint. I love that Job said, *"The Lord* takes away," and God's commentary is that Job didn't blame God or sin with his lips. It seems like a delicate line to walk. I hope we can do the same.

Forgive us if we don't answer calls, return text messages or Facebook things. We want to hear from you and receive your encouragement, but rarely have the energy to engage in a two-way conversation. So just know we appreciate it greatly, we love being loved, and what I'm writing now is about the best we can offer in return.

Before I leave off for now to go sit with Alice and watch "The Funny Guys" (her name for The Three Stooges), I sign off with the prayer my wife and I have prayed over and over:

So teach us to number our days
that we may get a heart of wisdom.
Return, O LORD! How long?
Have pity on your servants!
Satisfy us in the morning with your steadfast love,
that we may rejoice and be glad all our days.
Make us glad for as many days as you have afflicted us,
and for as many years as we have seen evil.
Psalm 90:12-15

Alice on a Florida beach, back in January

Chapter 16

A Day in the Life

As a father shows compassion to his children,
so the LORD shows compassion to those who fear him.
For he knows our frame;
he remembers that we are dust.
Psalm 103:13-14

April 25, 2018

This is not so much to give new information as it is to give a little window into what life is like for us and Alice these days. Mostly it's for us, so we can remember what it was like.

It's Tuesday evening, almost 9:00. I'm sitting at the kitchen table. Today's visitors have cleared out, and we're settling back into our normal. In the other room, I can hear Larry, Moe, and Curly poking, slapping, bonking, and insulting each other. "The Funny Guys," Alice calls them. The last two weeks or so, they've been her favorite. Mixed in is the sound of the kids and Shell, chatting, playing, now Natalie's making plans for a late grocery run. She's taken over the kitchen side of the domestic chores and has done a wonderful job. Now Joe, Emily, and Kylie have decided to tag along with her. Good for them, they need to get out and grab a breath of fresh air once in a while, even if it is a bit late.

Each of the kids has found a meaningful and helpful role in these days. Emily is, as always, Alice's go-to playmate. Kylie has become a nanny to Violet, and Joe facilitates any random whims Alice has to play video games, or helps handle little projects around the house.

It's all so mundane. And I don't mean that in a bad way. This is life for us, the life we love.

What do you do when your four-year-old is sent home with what is now down to 3-5 weeks to live? It's not something you practice for or think about. I suppose if I were to script it in a novel, I'd write it full of significant, meaningful moments like passionate hugs, long cries, soul-baring conversations, maybe even the occasional screaming "Why God?" into the midnight sky. I'd think maybe the days would have lots of family prayer, singing, Bible reading, meditations on heaven. You know, really spiritual-minded things. I'm a pastor, after all.

Those things do happen. Occasionally. Sunday morning we stayed home, and I took the time to walk us through what the Bible says concerning death, the divorce of soul from body, the role angels play in the lives of kids and in the transportation of souls from here to heaven, and finally we watched a video clip of Dr. Tom Schreiner walking through the theology of kids who die. It wasn't necessarily a time of mirth and merriment, but I hope amid the tears we were all fortified with great hope. We need a hope that won't let us down. The expected, but still disappointing recurrence of her cancer reminded us that all the other things we'd leaned on (treatments, nutrition, even hope for a miracle) were pretty flimsy. I'm thankful we didn't lean on them too heavily.

Mostly we're just living normal life. For us, that means meals, chores, maybe do some reading, some correspondence, sit with Alice while she plays, colors, eats, or watches The Funny Guys. Since she can't walk anymore, when she has to "wooz da baffroom," it involves some extra effort, but still, we feel privileged to serve her, even in that way.

While we're fully aware that we're getting down to the end of this chapter in our life, it's still difficult to emotionally grasp. Partly that's because with all we've been through, we've still never been through "the end." Partly it's because we've been living in this mode of impending tragedy for so long it feels "normal" and it's hard to think of what life was like without it, and partly because we just don't have much left in the way of emotions. I, for one, feel rather emotionally dead – like my ability to feel pain, sorrow, or grief has been depleted.

I remember back in September when this started, I cried for three days. Then I just couldn't anymore. When the news came last week, I cried for a day, but now I can't anymore. It's rather frustrating. I think perhaps one of the reasons I'm sitting down to write is perhaps to try to jump-start my soul again. I don't like the fact that my daughter is this close to the end of her life, and I can hardly feel anything. On second thought maybe I can feel something – I feel bad for not feeling.

On to other things... How's Alice?

Between April 13 and 20, Alice rapidly deteriorated, with each day bringing some new symptom. Sometimes it seemed as though we could see her change by the hour. Frightening. The day after her MRI, Dr. Chris called to say that upon reviewing her MRI in conference with other doctors, comparing it with her original one from September, it was possible that her symptoms might be somewhat relieved, temporarily anyway, through a certain treatment that had little to no side-effects.[13] We decided to give it a go, went to Children's on Friday for it, and after Saturday her slide seems to have stabilized somewhat. No improvements to speak of, but we haven't played the guessing game of "what's not going to work today?" for a few days.

Her right arm now has no function, and her left is rather shaky. She still likes to try to feed herself, and usually does pretty well. But she can get frustrated by the difficulty of picking up food or losing it halfway to her mouth, so Shelly developed a little game where she's the mama bird feeding Alice, the baby bird. It's fun and protects her dignity. This

---

[13] Turns out, this was a form of chemo-therapy. Because DIPG tumors sit behind the "brain blood barrier," chemo doesn't actually reach the tumor itself but gets filtered out, making it useless as a treatment against the tumor. So this wasn't meant to be in any way a cure.

morning eating waffles, I looked over and there's Alice with her mouth wide open going "tweet tweet!" Shelly fed her a forkful, then, with a mouth full of waffles, she flashed me a somewhat mischievous sideways grin that said something like, "I tricked Mom into doing my work!"

Her smile remains, at least so far, entirely unharmed and in near constant use. She's such a happy, content kid. Funny that she should be the one putting smiles on our face, but she is. I guess that's her contribution to the family life these days. Truth be told, it's been her contribution since she was born. She's just always been special that way.

About two weeks ago, she strung a blanket between the couch and love seat to make a tent, then put the mattress from the bassinet on the floor, took a blanket and a pillow inside, and called it her "blanket house." She sleeps there sometimes, including the last two nights. I sleep on the floor next to her (and boy do these old bones feel it!), but I'm not allowed to stick my head inside, unless it's to read Curious George before she falls asleep.

Speaking of which, she wants to sleep there again tonight, so Shelly and I are going to re-build it quick…

Done.

She's lying down, and I'm on the couch typing. She is kicking me through the blanket, laughing. Now she's complaining, "Some people are waking me up!"

You may recall that her eyes going out of alignment is what tipped us off to this thing in the first place. That's happened again, and sadly in a big way. She wears an eye patch most of the time, because otherwise her eyes get really strained trying to straighten themselves out.

Sometimes she drools a little, and that bothers her more than anything. The other day she said in disgust, "I spit like Violet!" Sometimes when she talks, she sounds exactly like my 90 yr. old Grandma did when she was suffering from ALS. Not always though.

She looks forward to the mail coming, and her eyes light up every day when there's something for her. So many people have been so unbelievably generous and kind, and she loves it all. Monday the kitchen table was full of packages.[14] FedEx, the mailman, and UPS all made a trip to the door with packages.

Alice has an unbelievably accurate mental inventory of her toys that is updated with every new addition, and her obsessive nature means if we can't find whatever certain little toy she's looking for, usually half the size of a golf ball, the only thing that comes out of her mouth is "Can you find my [whatever]?" until it's found.

Hospice came out to meet with us today. Those are sobering conversations. But as Michele and I had previously discussed, we've sort of made that mental switch from hoping and praying her life is spared, to hoping and praying her departure is easy for her, and that we will somehow not be ruined in the process. And I know many of the ones who love her have made that same transition in their thoughts and prayers as well. For what it's worth, we're ok with that.

If we were to even attempt to list all the really meaningful things friends, family, and strangers have done for and said to us, we wouldn't be able to scratch the surface. Just reviewing some of the comments left on the blog the other day I was reminded again of how much our little lady has done, and that without knowing it. We can hardly wrap our minds around the number of people praying for her; from Pastors crying their eyes out to little girls praying for Alice every night, from friends and family to people we've never met but who, in this world of amazing connectedness via social media, have fallen in love with Alice and found

---

[14] At the end of the previous post on the blog I had previously invited anyone to wished to send her gifts to do so. I struggled with all the generosity we received throughout this ordeal until I finally realized sometime around this time that it was kinder to the givers to let them do what they really wanted to do than discourage it under some pretense of humility. So it turned out to be lots of fun for Alice and I hope fun for those who were so eager to bring her happiness. The response was amazing; we were moved and she was indeed happy! I'm a slow learner but hopefully I can still learn.

themselves caught up in her story – we are so very grateful. To our Lewis Lake family, whatever I say to commend you will hardly be adequate to describe the love and care we've received from you. You are instruments in the hands of the God you serve, and you serve Him well. Bless you all.

Alice has fallen asleep for the night; it's time to grab some blankets and lay these old bones down next to her. We're told in all likelihood one day she'll fall asleep and just not wake up. We don't think that's gonna be tonight, but just in case, one of us wants to be there. And tonight "there" is on the living room floor, just outside the door of the "blanket house."

Chapter 17

Courage

I believe that I shall look upon the goodness of the LORD
in the land of the living!
Wait for the LORD;
be strong, and let your heart take courage;
wait for the LORD!
Psalm 27:13-14

May 7, 2018

Sunday night. The end of another day. It's nearly bedtime. Alice and Shelly are snuggling on the couch, watching The Funny Guys start a food fight at a party filled with high society types. Seventy years later, pies to the face are still funny.

It's been a good, good day. Emily and ten other kids from church were confirmed, and I couldn't have been prouder of my (once) little girl reading her treatise on the Trinity before a full sanctuary.

After the service little six year old Lindsey along with her little brother Brant, who attends Alice's 4-5yr old Sunday School class, came up to me holding a yellow can that said "Alice's Lemonade Stand" on it. Inside the can was $120 they'd made selling lemonade, and they wanted to give it to Alice. What a beautiful moment. Their mother was just a step behind them, crying what I presume was a beautiful combination of tears of joy over her children and sorrow over mine. I felt the same. These really are the best and the worst of times, and this moment illustrated it beautifully. So Lindsey and Brant, you're amazing. I squatted down to look the two young ones in the eyes and thank them and gave Lindsey a hug, but Brant wanted nothing to do with that. He's not a hugger, Lindsey informed me. So we did a fist bump instead. Love those sweet kids. Surely the Father in heaven sees the love and compassion these little ones have poured out on our Alice, and His heart is not unmoved.

When last I wrote, Alice was more or less holding steady. Eleven days later, that's still true.

I don't understand the workings of the brain, and even less a brain that's under siege from the worst grade of the worst tumor and the lingering side-effects of radiation, so I don't completely understand this second brief little "grace period" we're going through, and I don't think anyone knows how long it might last.

In the days following her last MRI, her health was failing precipitously. It was almost an hourly progression of symptoms. We went into a crisis mode. It's hard not to when you're sent home with such a brief window of time, rapidly failing health, and as a cherry on top, a bottle of concentrated morphine. This was followed by a visit from hospice, then a couriered delivery of seizure and anxiety meds that now occupies the space in the fridge just behind the milk.

But for the past two weeks now, from the outside anyway, her condition seems frozen in time. It's a strange thing to live through. When she was failing so fast, we said to each other "four to six weeks? It seems like she won't survive a week!" It seems like one involuntarily holds his/her breath when witnessing a calamity, and as Alice failed so rapidly right before our eyes, we held our breath. And held it. And held it. And after a while, like after two weeks, it's hard to hold your breath anymore! It's a strange kind of fatigue.

Forgive me if this sounds a bit insensitive, but maybe it will help illustrate how we feel. In the last few months I've occasionally described our situation to friends this way: It's like our daughter is having the time of her life playing in the street, and there's a truck about to run her over. Her shoes are frozen to the road and she can't get out of the way. We're standing on the sidewalk knowing it's coming, but are powerless to help and not really sure what exactly to say to her about it.

Many very well-meaning people have suggested we try various metaphorical crowbars, spatulas, or hot air balloons to lift her off the road, or recommended various shoe-unstuck experts, and it's not easy dealing with the reality that none of these could or would help.

We hoped and we prayed that the truck wouldn't come. But it came. And it hit her. Or, more accurately, *started* to hit her. Then it came to a sudden, unexpected stop. At some point it's going to start moving again. We just don't know when. Sooner rather than later I suppose. It all leaves us with an indescribably confusing and conflicting set of emotions. Again.

But those things aren't why I really wanted to write tonight. They're just necessary to answer the "How's Alice?" question.

Alice continues to bring a great delight to our lives. She faces this trial, no doubt with limited understanding, but also with great courage. And it's that courage that I wish to highlight, because I could, and hopefully do, learn much from my little Alice. Here's something of her courage:

Courage to be Content

By content I simply mean this: She's fully aware of the fact that her right arm should work. She should be able to walk. She shouldn't need an eye patch. Three weeks ago she was indistinguishable from just about any other typical 4-year-old. And she's not crazy about recent developments. But she doesn't complain, doesn't get frustrated, and has only asked "why" things aren't working maybe twice and been perfectly satisfied with the answer she's been given: "Honey, you've got some-thing making you sick. Jesus will fix it soon." She has switched to eating and writing left-handed, and you'd never know she's only been left-handed for two weeks.

Rather than complain, she rejoices in the things she can do. She can stand, if she slides off the couch keeping one hand on the coffee table, and when she does, she immediately looks to me for approval, smiling as big as if she'd just done a somersault. She's content to let us help her, she's content to help herself when she can.

The fact that she can't run, can only work half the controller on the X-Box (meaning a sister or brother has to run the other side, which they cheerfully do!), isn't able to uncap markers or play with her toys like she used to doesn't seem to bother her much. She's adjusted, fast and well. Her joy remains undiminished. She's content.

Courage to Trust

We had some breezy days this week, and someone sent us a kite. Kylie did the work of getting it flying, then Alice and I took over. As we lay on a towel in the yard, Alice held the string and I again began to talk with her a little bit about her future. Even if she never says anything, I know it bugs her that she can't walk. So as we watched the kite fly, I said to her, "Alice, someday Jesus is going to fix your legs and your sleepy arm and your eyes, and it's going to be great!" She comes up with the coolest names for everything, and "sleepy arm" is one of her best.

She smiled, sighed, and said happily and resolutely, "Jesus is going to fix my legs."

Her simple trust is a wonderful thing. She trusts her daddy. She's always trusted me to fix her broken stuff. Toys, games, swings, whatever is broken, she believes Daddy can fix it. That's my job. But I can't fix this one, and I told her that. But if Daddy says Jesus will fix it, she believes me, and she believes Jesus will fix it. And that's pretty awesome.

As God is faithful, after we both die I'm going to get to see her again. Because of that, I really do make a conscious effort to only give her hope I can ground in biblical truth. I'll be wrong about some stuff because I'm only human, but I'm guessing at that reunion she'll know the difference between me just making stuff up to make her feel better and doing my best to give her real hope. I'd hate for her to be disappointed in her Daddy for just spinning fairy tales when I should tell her the truth, because for better or worse, she believes everything I tell her. And someday she'll give me an earful if I steered her wrong!

Courage to Laugh

Alice is a funny kid. Sometimes on purpose, sometimes not. There's a lot of reasons *not* to laugh these days; Alice gives us lots of reasons *to* laugh. She told Pastor Bob today about seeing the giraffes when we went to Como Park one afternoon last week, telling him, "They stink!"

I came home last night after confirmation rehearsal, and Michele told me that she and Alice were cozying in bed when this little conversation took place:

"Mom, I'm sad. And Gob (God) is sad."

"Why are you sad? And why is God sad?" (Now at this point Michele is expecting something like God is sad because her legs or her "sleepy arm," don't work, she "sees two," or something along those lines.)

"Because we don't have any chips."

We have chips now.

Earlier this week she grabbed a marker and decided to draw on herself. She actually drew a pretty amazing stick person on her leg, considering she drew left handed and upside down. One thing led to another, and pretty soon she was drawing on everyone's face.

She scribbled all over Michele's face. She asked Alice, "What am I?"

"You're a dead cat."

Then, holding up her hand with her thumb and index finger almost touching each other, Alice smiled, peeked through the gap and said, "But a little bit alive."

Alice's cousin Tommy made family news last year when he ate an earthworm. Alice loves both Tommy and digging worms. So we dug some recently, and she decided to keep a couple as "a snack for Tommy."

Next time he came to visit, she excitedly gave him his "snack," and smiled and laughed as he dutifully chewed it up and gagged it down. No way he was going to let her down. Good stuff.

Speaking of worms, she also collected a bucket full of worms (and by "collected," I mean either Michele or I doing the digging, throwing worms toward Alice while she scoops them up with a big spoon, because there's no way she'll touch them!) and insisted that they go to "Mr. Larry," her fishing buddy. So Larry came by that night, bless his heart, to collect his bucket of worms, and then sat in his lap for an episode or two of "The Funny Guys." It was great to see them laugh together. Larry has invested much attention in Alice since our arrival at Quamba when she was barely a year old, and she loves him for it.

Courage to Give

While Alice has been the recipient of a *lot* of generosity, she also is very quick and eager to give. She loves to go shopping and asks us often to take her. When she finally charms me enough to load her up and take her (doesn't take long), her shopping list usually includes one thing for her, and something for her sisters, her brother, her cousins, aunts, uncles, grandparents, or who knows who else. So we wander the aisles as she sits in the floor of the cart, pointing the direction she wants to go, pulling various items off the shelves, looking it over, putting it back, until she decides what to get for everyone on her mental list. If she doesn't find what she's looking for, she says, "Dad, we can go to different store."

Good thing – I feared we were out of options! More aisles of pink! Ah well. We eventually find what we're looking for or something suitably close. Then we either deliver the goodies or whoever is to receive them will come over. She takes great delight in giving her presents. Pretty cool.

Before I close, I must once again give thanks to all who continue to pray for us. Many days are dark and hard; but every so often we get one that's happy and even, dare I say, "fun." And this Sunday was one of them, and we are so grateful. For all who have sent cards, letters, and gifts – bless you all. Each one is incredibly personal and thoughtful and meaningful, to Alice, and Michele and me. To the brothers in Michigan who have made it possible for my parents to be here and immediately available, thank you.[15] To the folks at Lewis Lake who have made it possible for me to just be home and do my part to lead my family through these difficult, often dark moments of life, thank you.

These are tough, taxing days, days when we often don't know what to do and don't have the energy to do it anyway. We are alternately restless and lethargic, sorrowing and rejoicing. God is good. He is faithful. He has not abandoned us. But this is hard. I've concluded that it's *supposed* to be hard. But we will accept good and bad from God's hand, because even and especially the bad things are working together for good. Our faith in God's plans for our good and Alice's good is renewed day by day. I firmly believe the Bible when it tells us that the joy that awaits us is in exponential proportion to the sorrows we feel now. Hope is a good thing, and we're so glad to have good hope.

---

[15] My Dad is pastor of Calvary Baptist Church in Negaunee, Michigan. The elders of the church encouraged him to take April and May in order to come to Minnesota. They stayed with my brother and were simply available for anything we needed. Yet another wonderful gift.

Chapter 18
Flickering

Yea, though I walk through the valley of the shadow of death,
I will fear no evil, ter you are with me!
Your rod, and your staff, they come ter me,
You prepared a table terfore me in the presence of my Emily's
You anoint my head with oil,
My cup (sipping sound) runs over.
Psalm 23:4-5, Alice's version

May 17, 2018

Twenty-nine days ago Dr. Chris told us "a month to six weeks." We're entering the window.

I would, of course, love to say he was way off. He would, I have no doubt, love to be proven wrong.

But doctors, though fallible, human, and hardly prophets in the truest sense of the word, are forced to live with and honor-bound to share what they know of reality based on both their extensive expensive education and real-life experience.

In other words, as much as I hate to say it, I'm not sure he'll be wrong. At least not by much.

The word I've used to encapsulate my own assessment of Alice the last couple of days is "flicker." That magnetic, infallibly loveable twinkle in her eye is still there. But not all the time. A weary, blank, far-away look occupies more time on her face now. Her sweet voice is still heard, but it is labored and slow, given in shorter, more deliberate sentences. Her wildly contagious, luminescent smile still lights up the room, but not as often.

A couple weeks back, when Joe and I took the Christmas lights off the house, rather than stuffing them into a bin like we probably should have done, we wrapped them around the trampoline netting instead. Eight or ten strings of lights looks pretty cool at night.

The day after my last writing was a beautifully warm day and evening, and after dark, Alice wanted to go lay down on the lit-up trampoline. The whole family went along with her. It was a warm night, and we've been gifted with lots and lots of blankets, so we threw a whole bunch of them on and visited, laughed, and had really a grand time together. Alice wanted to sleep out there too, so after Michele and Violet, Natalie and Joe went off to bed, she and I cozied on one side while Emily and Kylie crashed out on the other.

It occurs to me that I should explain something. Between sleeping on trampolines, under blanket houses, even occasionally good-naturedly (but rather firmly!) kicking me out of my own bed to the couch, one might get the impression that she's homeless within a home! So a quick clarification: Alice really does have a bed of her own. But she's careful not to wear it out. Her uniquely winsome presence and desirable companionship has meant she has always been not only welcome but highly sought after as a sleeping buddy. Even pre-dating cancer, she would invite herself to sleep with a sibling, or they would have good-natured competitions trying to get her to crash with them for the night. She'd sleep with Emily one night (or two... Emily being the favorite and all), then on Joe's floor the next, then with Kylie, with Natalie, and then repeat.

That night she picked me and the trampoline. It was fun for both of us, and even though we got a few sprinkles at 4:30 that morning, she slept right on through and got a good night's sleep. The other two girls bailed at some point during the night, while I slept off and on, greatly enjoying my Alice time.

The last couple days she's taken a fancy to hanging out under the chestnut tree in the yard. She decided the other day when she was out there that she wanted to "cozy Ducy." Lucy is a good dog, but hardly possesses a discriminating palette or decent sense of hygiene. That's a fancy way to say "she stinks." Which Alice discovered. She insisted on giving her a bath. So, tonight Alice and I washed Lucy. With SpongeBob soap, no less. Then Alice threw her blanket over the dog and thought it was the funniest thing in the world. How I love that laugh!

Alice has a little backpack that she packed up with some of her favorite toys because she wanted to go to "the little house and the little water." That roughly translates into a hotel and a pool.[16] We hadn't really talked to her about that or planned to do it, it was just her idea. After a week of asking Michele about it now and then, we decided to go for it and take her. Our window is closing, but she could still probably enjoy it, so yesterday we loaded up the youngest four and ran up to Duluth for a night at the Holiday Inn.

Her legs haven't been working great, but she was super excited to kick them in the pool, which she did, and laughed and laughed as she splashed Violet, who's a water-bug just like her older sister. Alice loved the hot tub, especially the bubbles (naturally!). It was lots of fun and totally worth the journey. But how quickly she tires these days. A few minutes of laughter, smiles, and fun, and then she's just out of gas. So we left the pool, went back to our room, and watched some more SpongeBob on "Daddy's 'puter." We're so grateful for so many generous people and a gracious church that make it financially and logistically possible to just up and bail out almost on a whim to maximize these days for her and for us.

Speaking of church, we've been able to bring her the last two Sundays. She loves going to church, and so many of her favorite people are there. Besides, she is showered with love and gifts when she's there, and who doesn't love that?

---

[16] In Alice lingo, "big water" is a lake or the ocean. "Little water" is a pool.

But last Sunday she wasn't able to enjoy it like usual. She didn't want to go to her Sunday School class, which was rather significant, because she loves her class and she loves Cheryl, her teacher. She just doesn't have the strength or the energy anymore. When we got home, Michele said to me, "I think that was Alice's last Sunday at church." Somehow I knew that was probably the case, but hearing her say it out loud hit me pretty hard.

That wasn't the only difficult thing we faced last Sunday. Thanks to social media and blogs, Michele and I have separately been following a small handful of other families with a child plagued by the same kind of cancer Alice has, at approximately the same stages. And for whatever reason, God only knows, the wheels for these dear ones seemed to fall off that weekend. Little Sophia down in Springfield, Missouri, Lea in Connecticut, Avery, and Eowyn all passed away. Down in Arkansas there's a girl named Addy. Her Daddy reached out to me several months ago to offer the hope they felt when the experimental treatments she received in Mexico seemed to be working. But he and his dear wife were crushed last week to find its effectiveness has run its course and the cancer rising up in greater and uglier ways than ever, and they've run out of options. Happy Mother's Day.

It's not easy to take when we've watched these dear folks and their kids live almost hauntingly similar lives to ours over the last few months, knowing our stories probably will continue to run parallel courses.

It was back in early January when Michele came to bed and said, "Molly died today." We never met Molly Worner, but her Mom kindly sent us some of her medicine to help ease the burns of radiation at the beginning of our journey. The Worner family Christmas card hung on our fridge for the longest time, and we think of them often, and they . continue to give us much encouragement.

We often read to Alice from a picture Bible sent to us by Kathryn Parsons' mom from out in New York. Kathryn's little body buckled under the weight of cancer not so long ago at the tender age of three. A couple weeks ago at bedtime (in Emily's bed that night, as I recall) I had the pleasure to read her the final chapter, Revelation 21-22, the description of heaven in kids language. It ends... "to be continued..." Kathryn's mom cheers us along too.

A year ago my friend Danyel buried her little seven year old Hannah, taken by cancer. I remember my wife reading me her story at the time and though I read lots of sad things – that's what happens when you get your news from the internet –I remember tears welling up because I knew Danyel and I knew what it was to love my girls, and my heart broke for her. And now I'm walking that same journey, just a step behind all these other ones. I suppose it's good to have company on this path, but I'd prefer this not be a path to begin with.

But it is. This is reality. It's not *all* of reality, but it is reality. Coming back to Dr. Chris and "a month to six weeks," I'm thankful he lives in reality and helps us know what it is, even when it's sucky. He doesn't get to ignore it. And we don't either. Lately my mind has been filled with thoughts of reality. Getting my head around what really *is*. I've been to funerals where the minister talked about the spirit of the departed floating about, and how that person would always live on in the hearts of those who loved him, and I can't help but think (hopefully not out loud), seriously? Is that what it's all about? Floating spirits and living on in my heart? I swear you're just making this crap up.

When staring at death, and I mean staring at it like we are, precious few people are pure materialists, that is, denying any sort of spiritual reality. Suddenly we *all* want to believe some part of a person keeps living in a world *somewhere*, that there is more to them than just their broken, dying body. Maybe sometimes matters of the immortal soul seem foggy, but death forces us to face the issue and by doing so helps to clarify our innate understanding that at the very least there's some fundamental, significant difference between the person we loved and the cow we ate for lunch at Arby's.

But I also have to say this: when I consider Alice's smile, the twinkle in her eye, her wavy hair, the looks she inherited from me, the personality she inherited from her mother, I don't want to be purely a spiritualist either. I love that dimpled smile, those twinkly eyes, and I'm crazy about the way she twirls her hair, not crazy about the way she picks her lips until they peel.

Alice is *more* than her little body and its aversion to my pokeys,[17] but that little body is very much *her*. And when it quits working, I want to know it's going to start working again.

The other day I buckled her in the van, and she threw her good arm over my neck, pulled my head down, kissed me on the nose (no whiskers there) and said, "I love you Dad. Dad? You can keep your pokeys." I love that. Spirits don't twirl hair and hate beards, at least not for the reasons Alice does. My sense from Scripture and reason is that when she leaves us, she won't be entirely happy until she twirls those same curls and smiles with those same eyes.

I want to be realistic because this is too important to just make stuff up so we feel better. If Dr. Chris looked at Alice's MRI and said, "Oh she's got 20 years left!" when he knew the truth, I'd be pretty upset with him. To be honest, I need to have the same (or greater!) level of confidence in what happens to Alice, to me, or to anyone who crosses that river into eternal life. I want to be confident my view of reality is a little firmer than making up a bunch of nonsense about floating spirits and the dead living on in my heart. I don't even know what that means! Much less do I have any faith that it's as real as my kitchen table. If Alice's life after death is contingent on her "living on in my heart," she's

---

[17] Her term for my beard. She never really liked me rubbing it against her face and would laugh and say "take off your pokeys!" I have a fun audio recording of one of those episodes, and treasure it greatly.

got a sketchy future, because my heart is a rather unreliable fountain of eternal life!

Reality. No games, no fairy tales. Truth. Something that won't disappoint, something that will actually turn out better than I could have even hoped for. This is my daughter; it's going to be me someday. It's going to be all my kids someday. Hopefully 80 years from now, but it's going to happen, sadly. When *it* happens, what happens?

We cling to Jesus. We do our best to steer Alice to Jesus. He offers us hope for both spirit and body. He's been dead; He's come alive again; He's still alive, and will be forever, just like I want Alice to be. I'd love for her to live to be 95. I'd far more love for her to just plain *never freaking die* and live in a better place than here. Jesus can do that. He promised he would. He died to make it possible. He lives because what is possible is now reality.

If the Bible isn't true, and if Jesus isn't raised, we Christians are the biggest fools in the world, in for the biggest disappointment ever. I get that. But it *is* true, and Jesus' tomb is empty, so we have reality, a good, solid, hopeful reality to enjoy. So we cling to Him; He'll not let us down.

And now we walk our little Alice "through the valley of the shadow of death." We see the tracks of those broken-hearted parents who have walked this road before us, and we hear their voices calling to us, "keep going, you'll make it." Bless you all for your help. When we reach the end, we can't take her across the river, but we can bring her to the shore, put her hand in His, and kiss her goodbye, for a little while.

Still, tonight is not yet goodbye, just goodnight.

Chapter 19
Dishonor

"I didn't think I could love her more,
but now that her eyes are crossing and she can barely move…
I love her more." – Michele

We rejoice in hope of the glory of God.
Not only that, but we rejoice in our sufferings,
knowing that suffering produces endurance,
and endurance produces character,
and character produces hope,
and hope does not put us to shame… Romans 5:2b-5a

May 28, 2018

*I*t's hard for me to write if I feel that nothing particularly noteworthy has happened worthy of recording or reading. It's not that nothing has happened, it's just that what is happening is moving along in slow motion. Of course, in retrospect we may look back at these days and feel they were like living in a hurricane. But as it stands now, it's just a grueling process. The number of times we thought it would be over within a matter of days is only equaled by the number of times we felt it would drag on in perpetuity.

The word I used to describe Alice a few weeks ago was "flickering." Tonight I might use the word "fading." The light in her eyes continues to dim. Her legendary smile, not yet entirely relegated to the realm of memory, is but a shadow of its former glory.

However, I want to take a risk and rather than using safe and benign description of "fading," the word that more fully encapsulates her in these moments is "dishonor."

I take the word from the Apostle Paul who, referring to the death and burial of a Christian said, "We are sown in dishonor..."

Alice's tumor is not only sucking the life out of her, it's stripping her of her dignity. She tries to draw pictures like she once did, but she's frustrated by her inability to make her unsteady hand do what she wants it to do, and she hates that her drawings aren't nearly as good as they used to be. She needs help in the bathroom. She drools, a lot. Every word is laborious, slow and increasingly unclear. Her once sparkling eyes are crossed and she struggles to focus them (although... eating nachos this afternoon she managed to spot on one of her chips a molecular sized piece of ground beef that had to be removed before she would eat it!) And I don't think it has gone unnoticed that her 9-month-old sister is more mobile than she is.

This slide into dishonor is hard to watch. After all, I deeply desire her to be honored, to be glorious, free from being humbled by a disease we can do nothing about.

On the one hand the worse she gets, the more love and compassion we feel for her. It doesn't matter how weak she is, how sparse the laughs or slow the words, our love transcends those things, is even intensified by them. There are hidden dimensions of love that can only be revealed when a certain kind of light is shining. As Michele said, we "love her more," because we love her in new and different ways we simply couldn't before. There's something to be learned about God's love for us by observing Michele's love.

On the other hand, if we were able, *of course* we would restore her beauty and her abilities to their original form. So there's both a sense in which it doesn't matter that she is being dishonored by cancer and another in which it very much *does* matter, because we want the dishonor gone and the beauty of vitality back.

After all, every citizen of heaven will be made glorious, honorable, and beautiful. Ugliness, deformity, and incapacity will all be eternally transformed into stunning and satisfying perfection. Imagine an eternity of life with flawless beauty, untouched by age, sorrow, or disease. Dignity, honor, and beauty matters to God. Dishonor will be banished in heaven. Those sown in dishonor, said the Apostle, will be raised in glory. That means Alice's twinkly eyes will return; her laugh will again fill the room, that glorious smile will once again reproduce itself on every face that witnesses it.

Tonight she is still with us. And we're glad. We get to hang out under the chestnut tree just a little bit more. How much longer, who knows. Maybe days, maybe weeks. Tuesday will mark the end of week six since the 4-6 week prognosis. Alice is very, very tired. Her breathing is getting faster, her heart is working harder. She is getting weaker. I wish it wasn't so.

This week I sensed the entire family was getting really weary of the battle. This is a hard thing to live through day after day. So I wanted to try to provide some bit of relief. You know, get out of the house and do something fun. But it dawned on me with force and frustration that Alice really can't get out anymore and that makes me incapable of doing those diversions that sort of refresh our energies. There's not much that's "fun" for her either out and about or even right here at home. She may be able to muster up the strength to enjoy something for a few moments, but that's about it. She's just tired. Tonight she had a few moments of fun sitting on the trampoline with a marker scribbling on everyone else's face or arms or legs. Kind of a shame we'll have to wipe it off.

Michele and the kids continue to amaze me. I'm in awe of Michele's strength in these days. She maintains her poise and stability while loving and hurting more deeply than I can even imagine. The kids have adapted so well to this alternate universe we've found ourselves in the last eight months. I am so very proud of all of them. God give us continued grace.

I remain confident that God has heard our prayers. I hope to write about that soon. I remain adamant that the day is coming when we will see with eyes filled with tears of gratitude that this is the best thing that ever could have happened to her, and to those who love her. It's really the only way to make sense of the inescapable three truths that (1)nothing happens except that which God is in control over, (2)He loves her more than we do, and (3)He is perfectly capable of fixing her at any moment (and has been begged to do so repeatedly and loudly by a great multitude!) and hasn't yet chosen to do so. For those God loves, all things, even and especially the bad ones, work together for good. He loves, and He works. That has to be enough for us for now.

If I think of what I would do for her with my limited love and limited ability, imagine what God is doing and will do for her with His infinite love and infinite abilities. And for that reason, we trust Him with these moments of dishonor. They are temporary. They are producing for her an eternal weight of glory. I'm not crazy about the process, I'll admit. But I am really excited about seeing what God makes of it.

We continue to be the recipients of unbelievably kind, gracious, and thoughtful generosity, more than we could ever hope to begin to acknowledge. A few months ago, I used to take Alice with me into the Wells-Fargo in Cambridge when I had to do something at the bank. She only accompanied me inside because she knew they have suckers. It turns out that the lady who helped me set up Alice's savings account there is also my neighbor. So after I got to know Tricia a little bit, I would send Alice into her office to steal suckers whenever we were at the bank. For the last six weeks, Tricia and her kids have dropped a sucker in our mailbox for Alice every day without missing a single one. Amazing. If you can't find a pink sucker at the bank, it's because Alice gets them all. Tonight, I had to say that Alice just can't do suckers anymore. I hated having to do that!

For all the cards, letters, and gifts, on Alice's behalf, I offer you her thanks. I only wish you could enjoy her enjoying them. For all the prayers for her and for us, thank you. We need them, and they buoy our hearts. To our Lewis Lake family, and Pastor Bob, who continually support and encourage us along, who gave their hearts to Alice knowing full well it might break them to do so, thank you.

Chapter 20
Walking Through the Valley

For he delivers the needy when he calls,
the poor and him who has no helper.
He has pity on the weak and the needy,
and saves the lives of the needy.
From oppression and violence he redeems their life,
and precious is their blood in his sight.
Psalm 72:12-14

June 7, 2018

J ust wanted to give a quick update on Alice.

Sunday night Alice suddenly started making seal noises, her breath came in short fits, and because it came on instantly, it scared the living daylights out of us. A call to hospice led to an ambulance ride, and by about midnight the episode had cleared, and we returned home about 1AM.

It's interesting to sit in the ER chatting with a doctor about treating a child who is so near death's door. Typically the goal of medical care is "Let's get you back flying high again!" But for Alice these days it's more like, "Let's try to crash this plane more gently."

Her almost complete inability to swallow leads has predictable, but really difficult effects. To say "it sucks" is the understatement of my lifetime.

Monday night marked the beginning of a terrible period for Alice, and for us. I'll draw the curtain of modesty around most of those 36 excruciating hours as she gasped for breath, our medical options exhausted, while we were simply left feeling entirely helpless while our daughter was at the mercy of her cruel, cancerous tyrant. Perhaps that sounds a bit dramatic, but in the moment, that's how it felt. Suffice to say, you wouldn't want to see it in your mind's eye, and I don't want it replayed in mine.

Jesus cried on the cross "Why have you forsaken Me?" Theological implications aside for the moment, it occurred to me that when we tell God we're okay with death, there's this expectation that He's going to reward our submission to His will by making the process as easy as possible. Surely, even in death He wouldn't allow His loved ones to go through hours of seemingly unnecessary suffering? When He does, it truly feels like abandonment. We've long since made our peace with the reality of having to say goodbye to Alice; we weren't quite . prepared for the process leading up to the hand-off to be so difficult, and it felt like God wasn't showing up to soften the blow, hold our hand, draw near, and meet our expectations of a peaceful, quiet transition this life to the next. After all Lord, it's for Alice,. Why must she suffer misery on top of misery?

I wrestled hard with God in those hours. I watched my wife's heart be torn to pieces before my very eyes. For months we begged him to heal Alice; he chose not to. Then as she struggled hour after hour, unable or unwilling to sleep, we exhausted all our available medical options with nothing left to do but simply hold and comfort her. We begged Him to take Alice home. He wouldn't do that either.

Thankfully that dark period has passed, and a new day has come, just like we were promised. Alice has been resting quite peacefully for the last day and a half. If she's peaceful, we're peaceful. If you know where to look, you can still see her under the cover of crippling cancer and medication. Though far too weak to set on the potty, she's still too proud to wear a pull-up, and summons every ounce of strength left to tell us she'll have none of it. Nobody is going to put a cup of juice to her lips – if she can't hold it, she don't want it.

We've had a steady trickle of family around for the last couple of weeks, and so thankful for them and for our parents' willingness to traverse the many miles required to be at our beck and call. Tuesday evening at my request, my family came *en masse* to say goodbye. She was happy to see them, especially her favorite cousins and Uncle Keith, the only other person with the same profound appreciation for sitting down to a bag of M&M's and The Funny Guys as she does. Lots of sorrowing, but not as those who have no hope. Pastor Bob came and ministered deeply and sweetly to our hearts in a way we really needed after those hard couple of days.

I don't know how much longer Alice will be with us. Truth be told, I expected her to be gone Monday night. The well of life in her is very deep, and until she's ready to do a thing, it probably won't be done. That's just her way. She's probably rather weary of being kissed on the cheek – how well do I remember some months ago when she would demand, "No more kisses!"

I don't think she can see much anymore, but she sure likes when I lay my phone next to her and play The Funny Guys. And she loves having her siblings around. As I write, Emily is lying beside her discussing some of the finer points of playing dolls. For Alice, it's a little piece of pre-heaven. I've admired my kids all throughout this journey, but they have shone particularly bright these last few days. We are experiencing grace; it just pops up where we're not always looking.

Thank you for your prayers. In the darkest hours of this storm, when we most felt like our Father had abandoned us, knowing and hearing that He has moved so many of you to pray for us was perhaps the only balm for our weary, troubled souls. Thank you for praying for us when we've felt unable to pray. We have been greatly shaken, and the fires of this trial have burned away some of our more romantic ideals of how God relates to His children in hard times, but the foundation of God's Fatherhood is firm. We wonder for Alice and for us, "if this is light, momentary affliction, what must the eternal weight of glory look like?" I'm not sure entirely, but it'll be awesome. I expect Alice will know a little more than I do real soon.

Alice & Aslan

Drawn by Michele, and now hanging in my office.

Chapter 21
Alice in the Palace

My frame was not hidden from you,
when I was being made in secret,
intricately woven in the depths of the earth.
Your eyes saw my unformed substance;
in your book were written, every one of them,
the days that were formed for me,
when as yet there was none of them.
Psalm 139:15-16

Consider… the happy condition of a Christian! He has his best things last, and therefore in this world he receives his worst things first. But even his worst things are "later" good things, hard plowings yielding joyful harvests.

— Spurgeon, ed. by Alistair Begg

June 9, 2018

Back during radiation days when Alice was on steroids, she was insatiably, obnoxiously hungry. All she could think about was eating. She would close her eyes at night dreaming of breakfast, and end each meal asking for more. There was no reaching "full" on her tummy gauge. I remember it was so hard trying to calm her down while she was miserably obsessing about food.

Then we discovered the word "later." Alice, you can have more Cheerio-Bear *later*. You can have "crispus chicken" *later*. Yes, you can have noodles *later*. And wouldn't you know it, it actually worked. She would say, "ok," and for while anyway, that was that. She trusted us that the food was coming, and so long as the promise was there, she could, and did endure.

I was always surprised that it worked. But so long as we held up our end of the deal and "later" actually came, she was ok with putting up with a little misery in the present for some happiness in the future. She learned to work the system, too. "Dad, can we go to the store?"

"Not now honey."

"Dad, we can go to the store *later*."

"We sure can, Alice. And we will"

Once she got my word, she made sure I didn't forget. Later always came.

For 8-1/2 months now, we have been keenly aware that our Alice gauge never gets quite full. You just can't get enough Alice. Her smiles, giggles, her funny phrases, her winsome presence that just made life better because she was there in it. The more Alice life had in it, the sweeter it was. If you knew Alice, or even if you've just seen her pictures and gotten to know her a little bit through the dim glass of my words, you know this to be true.

And so we have asked our Father for more Alice. Last night He said, "*Later*."

As Alice trusted her "later" to Mama and Daddy, and in our imperfect, failing ways we tried to deliver, we now look to our Father fully expecting him to deliver.

Alice is in the Palace. A little after 9:00 I was lying beside her in bed, alternately doing a little reading, staring into those tired eyes that could no longer close or open, stroking her hair, comforting Emily who was crying as she lay on the other side of her. I noticed her breaths became incredibly shallow. At the piano, Michele had just finished playing "*God be with You Till We Meet Again*." I called her in, and the kids all came in, and we gathered around, lifted Alice into Shelly's arms and together we watched and cried as Alice drew her final breaths. I lay my head on Alice's chest and heard her little heart, which had been pounding like a hammer for several days, fade into silence. At 9:13, she was gone. We kissed her, cried over her, recited Psalm 23 together, and thanked our Lord for giving her to us. Better to have just a few short years of Alice time than none at all.

In the end, Alice died peacefully. I never would have believed she had the strength to endure as long as she did. There is so much more to her than we knew, even though knowing her as thoroughly as we could has been such a central part of our life these last months.

I sent a quick text to the aunts, uncles, cousins, and grandparents: "Alice is in the Palace. The Lord has given, and the Lord has taken away. Blessed be the name of the Lord." Quickly and quietly, they once again reassembled at our house, Pastor Bob came, and we gathered around Alice, still lying there in our bed. We hugged, cried, and listened to Pastor Bob speak to us words of hope and comfort, the sweet promises of a loving Heavenly Father.

I had decided several months ago that if Alice must go, I wanted to build her coffin, or as I call it, her final bed. It just seemed right, and something I could do to honor my daughter. I guess I've always made most of the beds and furniture around our house, and I didn't want her sleeping in a bed someone made when I could make it.

It seemed wrong to be building it while she was awake, and I really didn't want the other kids to know what I was doing, so one Friday night shortly after her cancer returned, about 11:00, my brothers and brother-in-law came, and together we worked all night to build it, finishing up just after the sun came up Saturday morning. I really hoped she'd never have to use it, but now that she needs one last bed for her weary body, I'm glad to be able to give it to her. And I'm so grateful to these fellow carpenters for coming to tackle it with me. It was a great honor to watch them ply their tremendous skills on such a strange project at such a strange hour. I think I'll always think fondly of working together with them that night, hard as it was.

I feel like there should be an "end credits" or something, like this is the end of Alice's story so I need to give thanks to everyone who made it what it was. Let me just say this, and I hope it suffices: Alice received more love and support from more people and places than any little girl could ever have dreamed. And because Michele and the kids and I were so near her, we got splashed, no, we were drenched by the deluge of love that you all have poured out on Alice. Thank you. Thank you to the people at the "doctor's house" that she loved so much, thank you to our church family who continually encouraged me to just keep my eyes on Alice and made it possible for me to spend more time with her than I could have ever imagined. Thank you to all who prayed her and us through this – I will say more to you hopefully in the near future – and thank you all who sent cards, money, and gifts, like little beams of light on our dark path that lifted our spirits, eased our burdens, and nourished our bodies and souls. Thank you to our families, friends, and church that have allowed their lives to be interrupted so many times to care for Alice and us.

And to the Lord Jesus, we thank you in faith, believing today as always that you have orchestrated this in such a way and for such a purpose that *later* we will give thanks and really *feel* thankful. We are thankful for so much goodness from Your hand, but truth be told, right now we'd trade the goodness we've seen while losing Alice for just not losing her in the first place. We trust you.

As I thought about the imagery of Psalm 23 last night, particularly the green pastures, the table in the presence of the enemies, and an overflowing cup, I couldn't help but imagine Jesus and Alice having a bit of a picnic under some celestial chestnut tree in the front yard of the Palace, her tumor lying lifeless and now harmless before them, Alice laughing as Jesus fills her celestial cup until it overflows and just keeps pouring and pouring and pouring… I know she arrived thirsty. Anyway, as they raise their dripping glasses, Alice smirks and gives that wretched cancerous blob a slap and a poke, Funny Guys style. Surely goodness and mercy has followed her, and she will dwell in the house of the Lord forever. Can't wait to join her.

Chapter 22

Honor

Devout men buried Stephen
and made great lamentation over him.
Acts 8:2

Pay to all what is owed to them:
Romans 13:7-8

June 16, 2018

*I*t's approaching 11:00, Friday night. The house is a filled with a veritable potpourri of fragrances emanating from the flowers from Alice's funeral. Flowers on the table, flowers on the piano, flowers on our dresser, flowers on just about any piece of furniture that will hold a basket or a vase. I won't attempt to put my ignorance of botany on display and name them or give credit to which ones smell nice, other than to say there's roses, lilies, and lots of other ones that Shelly could identify. I just know they're pretty. But I can't really escape the nagging thought that while tonight we're surrounded by such beauty, in a few days these things will all have wilted away, and we'll have to get rid of them. Seems like the sad echo of an unpleasant song we've heard before…

We miss Alice. All of us do. Her absence makes our table feel empty and our dinner conversations lacking the necessary voice to make them complete. One of the kids put a SpongeBob DVD going this evening, maybe more for the familiar background noise now synonymous with Alice than to enjoy the comedic genius. Her death has, predictably and unsurprisingly, left a huge hole in our family. And that's as it should be.

The week leading up to the funeral was a mixture of having both too many things to do and not enough. Saturday morning we went to the funeral home and started hammering out details for the service. Because this moment didn't come as a real surprise to us, and Michele and I occasionally talked about it in the days and weeks leading up to it, we had most of the big things figured out, which was helpful. But still, there was a number of details to figure out, decisions to make, and papers to sign. Some form of mental autopilot took us through most of it.

Our primary aim in putting the service together was to see our faithful God and beloved Alice honored, each in their proper way. We actually didn't have to do very much because all of the heavy lifting was done by those who loved us. We just kind of laid out our vision for what we wanted, and were surrounded by willing hands and loving hearts who made it all happen.

Over the past months, we often heard the words "If there's anything I can do, please just tell me!" My most common response became, "I wish there was something you could do; I wish there was something *I* could do!" That wretched feeling of helplessness that we all felt during the last leg of this journey was hard. But that changed when Alice went to the Palace. Suddenly there was lots to do, we needed lots of help doing it, and that was in some respects refreshing.

My sister-in-law Miranda was in charge of putting pictures together. It's almost emotional suicide in these moments to relive Alice's life as one sorts through the thousands of pictures we have of the brief time we enjoyed her presence. Besides, Alice couldn't take a bad picture. She had her mom's photogenic nature – the camera loved her. Alice's slide show was 455 pictures and almost 37 minutes long. The first time we watched it at home, we all cried our eyes out. But we've found that reliving the happy moments through pictures has helped to recalibrate, to some degree, our memories of her. We don't want to forget the ugliness of the final weeks of Alice's life, but we certainly don't want that to be the only thing we remember. Pictures help sort that out a lot.

My three siblings and I have a (mostly) unofficial but very solemn agreement between us – we won't discipline each other's kids, and we won't allow what my sister years ago coined "barf on a biscuit" at each other's funerals. As if funerals aren't sad and disappointing enough, only to endure to the end and be rewarded with... ground bologna! It's like insult to injury. So I knew I could trust Ginny with taking care of the food.

She graciously took on the responsibility, and her and the ladies from Lewis Lake made it happen in a wonderful, kid-friendly, Alice-honoring way.[18] They faced a pretty monumental task; putting together a meal planned for 450 people is hardly a simple affair, but they made it happen. Dickey's in North Branch did the meat. Rumor has it the owner discovered what the order was for, and went far above and beyond in honor of Alice. We are so thankful. That's actually one of the last places we bought chicken for Alice, and she really loved it.

Because of the anticipated size of the group, we had been presented with the option of checking into using the school where we did the benefit last year, but Pastor Bob and I both agreed that, inconvenient though it may be, the church is the proper place for something like this. So our dear Lewis Lake family willingly and cheerfully (their *modus operandi* for service, I should note...) went about the business of getting a building designed to handle 250 people prepared for a gathering of 550. They borrowed chairs from another church, squeezed them in wherever they could, put video feeds together into overflow rooms, and who knows what else. Our offers to help were flatly declined. Maybe behind

---

[18] I invited parents to bring their children to Alice's funeral. Not wanting to waste any of this trauma, I thought it was a wonderful opportunity for children to come face to face with death while accompanied by men I could trust to help interpret that experience for them. I wasn't disappointed, and believe it will bear much fruit.

our back they winked and said that great line from *A Bug's Life,* "Help us… don't help us!"

Thursday morning we arrived at the church about 20 minutes before visitation began, briefly greeted some of our family who had already arrived, made our way to my office to briefly pray, sort of compose ourselves, and then together we made the long march up to see Alice.

She was laid on a pillow and blanket made by her Great-Grandma. She loved it so much and always called it her "Gramma Rosie blanket." She was wearing her favorite kitty tights, pink shoes, and blue flowery dress. Alice always wore dresses, and once when I wondered aloud why that might be, "Miss Cheryl" explained, "Princesses don't wear pants."

I think it was easier to see her than we expected. Michele said the only thing out of line was that her hair was too perfectly done – in life it was always a bit of a mess. So I tousled it up just a little, but she scolded me for my efforts. I think she was secretly happy I did it though, because Alice looked even more like Alice. It was a precious moment there, all eight of us together one final time. I know it's proper to say Alice wasn't there, and while that's true in one sense, it's also true that her body is her too, so as Alice might say, she really was there "little bit."

If honor can be measured by the greatness of the crowd, the greatness of the people in the crowd, and the greatness of the effort to be there, Alice was indeed honored, and we were so happy to see it so. The place was packed, and it was packed with honorable men of God, well-respected businessmen, men and women of great integrity, and pillars of the church and community. Maybe it's not saying much, but I say there was more honor and dignity attendant at Alice's funeral in the middle of the sticks in Central Minnesota than a state funeral held in Washington DC.

We often say in moments like these, "it's a shame we only get together at such a time as this." But it occurred to me on Thursday that not many moments are worth making the effort required to be together. It's hard to set work aside for a day and sometimes multiple days in order to be present at such an event. But so many did. And great men and great women, people of high stature not simply in our hearts, but the eyes of everyone, made their way to pay respect to our Alice. We were so deeply moved, and she was greatly honored. It did my Daddy's heart much good.

For almost two hours, Michele and I stood near Alice, greeting, hugging, and sometimes crying with family and friends. They were precious moments for us, and each person infused a little joy or very sweet and fitting sadness into our hearts. I lifted some of Alice's young friends up so they could see her, and thanked them for loving her and being her friend. That was, to me, one of the highest honors of my day. We still didn't get to see everyone, and not everyone got to see Alice, and that's a bummer. But how great to greet childhood friends, people I've worked with, people we've ministered to and with, and friends and family from near and some from very far. The day was a wonderful mixture of the sadness of separation and the joy of reunion. I suppose it's another metaphor.

Just before the service began, my kids once again assembled with Michele and me around Alice's little bed, pulled the blanket over her little body and tucked her in one last time. Shelly folded over a corner so it looked just perfect, and my son and I, the men of the family, closed the lid.

Ivan Fiske read Rev. 21:1-7 with a voice and a passion that can only come from the heart of a man who actually believes what he's reading. My Dad delivered a beautiful, God-centered eulogy, the pastor in him making much of Jesus and the Papa in him making much of Alice. At our request, Ben and Rachel came from Michigan to sing, and they did so beautifully. My Grandparents weren't able to attend, but they had seats reserved just behind us, so we gave one to one of my oldest friends, the one and only Bear. How his tears honored our girl, and how our hearts were uplifted to hear that famously rich and powerful baritone singing with us and the congregation, *"Day by day, and with each passing moment, Strength I find to meet my trials here, Trusting in my Father's wise bestowment, I've no cause for worry or for fear..."*

Pastor Bob invited all the kids up to the stage where he shared with them about "old things that wear out, and new things that are broken." These are incredibly powerful moments in the hearts of kids, to be carefully and properly handled, and they really were. I couldn't believe how many kids were in attendance, it was super cool and again, made me so happy. As they were coming off the stage, one little girl came up to Bob and said, "But I didn't get to see Alice!" She was heartbroken, and I was for her. For a moment I thought about taking her hand and opening up the lid for her, but it just seemed improper, so I just smiled as Bob kindly told her we'd have to wait until we would see her another day.

We raised the roof with *"In Christ Alone,"* and Bob preached about the death that glorifies God. It was just wonderful, and we were so pleased.

After the benediction, we followed as Alice was wheeled out then lifted by our brothers, our dads, and Pastor Ivan into the coach. We followed as she was slowly driven around the church building to the cemetery in the backyard, where those men of honor and dignity once again lifted her up and carried her to her final resting place. We stopped, turned toward the people who were following us, and watched as wave after wave of people came around the church building and into the cemetery, a beautifully huge crowd gathered around a little wooden box.

Shelly wanted a balloon launch, so we turned the preparation for that project over to her cousins. Who knew there's a helium crisis going on in the US? But nothing really stops the Anderson clan from getting the job done, so by hook or crook I suppose (I don't ask and they don't tell), they made it happen.

When we stepped outside the building after the service, Jojo had our family's seven big red balloons in hand and tried to pass them out to each of us. I didn't feel like taking one at the moment so I told him to just hang on to them. It was windy, so by the time we walked from the church door to the graveside they were so tangled together there was no separating them. So he launched them for all of us. In retrospect, I kind of like the imagery of our family balloons being inseparably bound together by the working of the wind. It's a metaphor…

Watching 300 balloons float off was incredible, and all the kids had a blast sending them off. I was amazed at how fast they all disappeared. Another metaphor, I suppose.

After the launch, Bob spoke briefly, we prayed the Lord's Prayer, and once again committed her little soul and body into the hands of the only One who ever could help her, and ultimately the only One who can help us.

It was a beautiful afternoon, and we lingered around the grave, sharing more hugs and more pleasant words with those we love and who love us. I finally got to meet Pam, the dear lady who weekly mailed Alice a box or boxes full of gifts, which she always tailored to fit Alice's changing condition. She's brilliant. I dearly wish Pam could have met Alice to see how much joy she brought to her. The love of this lady for my daughter she never met was so moving.

It occurred to me sometime this week that from the moment I carried Alice's body out of our house and lay her down in the back of that shiny black van almost one week ago to the hour, she was always in the hands and under the care of people who knew and loved our family. Because I've officiated several funerals, I have had the pleasure of knowing and working with the funeral director and his assistants. Josh, who digs most of the graves in the area, attends Lewis Lake and his daughter Lydia was in Alice's Sunday School class. And of course Alice even now sleeps in a bed made by her Daddy and her uncles. Somehow it was a comforting thought that she was never in the hands of strangers.

In a rather unexpected twist of events, the only stranger that eventually did happen to enter the equation was the fellow who was in charge of lowering her bed into the ground, in common parlance "the vault guy." When he set up the mechanism to lower her bed into the ground earlier in the day, he didn't realize it was a child-sized box,[19] so the straps used to lower her were set up too far apart. So there was a bit of labor involved resetting the rigging used to lower her down, including removing the box from above the grave momentarily while things got adjusted properly. No doubt he was, like other professionals would be, overjoyed to have to try to correct the problem in front of and with the assistance of Alice's family and friends (just a little sympathetic sarcasm from one working man to another). But it was actually really meaningful to me to be a part of helping with the last 6 feet of her journey.

The concrete lid of the vault makes a rather ominous sound when it literally slams into place. But it's just lying there, not fastened down. I didn't put a latch on the lid of her bed either. I suspect she'll just float up through it, but in the event that on resurrection day she decides to push her way out, maybe she'll smile when she realizes her Daddy made it as easy as possible to escape that thing. Or maybe she'll roll her eyes and think I was in too much of a hurry to finish the thing right.

Alice and I used to play a game where I'd hide my wedding ring or piece of candy in one of my hands and she would guess which hand it was in. No joke, I bet she was right 90% of the time. To this day I don't know how she did it, but it always amazed me. Then she would put my ring in her hand and say in a musical way, "Which one?" and if I guessed

---

[19] I was generally pretty intentional about saying "Alice died" instead of something more gentle, like "Alice passed away" or "Alice went to heaven," because I didn't want to try to make it less awful than it was. However, for some reason I couldn't quite spit out the word "coffin." Instead I used "bed" and even "box," as here. Eventually I worked up the courage to use the word, see ch. 25.

right, as quick as she could, she would put her hands behind her back and switch the ring to the other one, put them forward again, and triumphantly open her empty hand. It was a losing game for me, and I loved it. I'll miss it a lot. I already do.

We don't know what life will be like for us going forward. Sorrowing yet rejoicing, I expect. We're still in the process of feeling a hundred different and conflicting things all at once. I like to say that if we had to go through the last 8-1/2 months all over again, there's some things we would do differently, but we have no regrets. As best we were able, we have mentally prepared for this day while hoping we'd never see it. We hoped God wouldn't take her, but I don't think either of us would say we are surprised that he did. We don't know *why* He did, and even though the good that we've seen come of it is significant, it hasn't yet equaled what we think she's worth. Still, we know that one day we will be vindicated when we say that He does all things well.

More than anything in the world, I want my kids, all of them, to spend eternity in the joyous presence of the Lord Jesus. I care far less *how* they all get there than *that* they get there. Alice made it. Counting her miscarried siblings, for us that's five there, five to go. God bring the rest of us safely home. The other kids are doing so well and have made us both so very proud. They're the best, and though they have been bent over and bowed down while being battered by this storm, for them and for us the saying is true, "*A bruised Reed He will not break.*" (zing!) Turns out God never promised us as smooth sailing as we might have desired. But the promises he has made us have so far been well kept.

He gives and takes away. Blessed be the name of the Lord.

A little "Alice in Wonderland" photo op, featuring a genuine

Alice and the amicable and highly cooperative Steve the Rabbit

Chapter 23
The Vault of Unanswered Prayers

You have kept count of my tossings;
put my tears in your bottle.
Are they not in your book?
Psalm 56:8

June 22, 2018

Statistically speaking, children who develop Diffuse Intrinsic Pontine Glioma, or DIPG, have a 0% chance of surviving for five years after diagnosis. On average, the time between diagnosis and death is nine months.

Alice was diagnosed with DIPG on September 23, two days before her fourth birthday, and died eight and a half months later, on June 8th. From a medical perspective, her journey was more or less textbook. Diagnosis, radiation, a few happy months of remission, a disappointing if predictable recurrence, death.

From the beginning of her journey, Alice's name echoed in the halls of heaven as hundreds and even thousands of people begged God to release her from the grip of her cancer. The sheer vastness of the army of God's people storming the Throne of Grace was baffling to me; the only conclusion I could reach is that God Himself moved His people to pray. So, we prayed. Just like God moved us to do. We begged God to do what only He could do. DIPG has no survivors. We had no hope in medicine, but in God there is always hope, and besides, He inspired us to pray.

And then, without the slightest hint of any supernatural intervention at all, Alice died.

What difference did it make that all those prayers were offered? What sense does it make that God moved His people to pray, only to refuse their requests?

I have wrestled with those questions throughout this ordeal, as perhaps many of you have, and what follows is my train of thought on the matter. I hope the conclusion will be as encouraging to you as it has been to me.

God is in Control

I begin by recognizing the truth that not only does God *know* the end of human history as well as the beginning, He has *designed* it, both in the main and in the details. This leads me to the uncomfortable conclusion that God wasn't surprised by Alice's cancer, rather He had actually ordained it to be so.

Now this is a hard pill to swallow. Especially at first. But as far as I can tell, it's the only way to make sense of the reality that God not only knows everything that *does* happen, he knows everything that *might* happen. Or as theologians say, God knows all things *actual* and *potential*. So even if we recoil at the notion that at some level God would actually design the death of little girls into the fabric of history, at the least we have to say that He could have set into motion a sequence of events that would prevent it from happening.

If we, quite understandably, want to say that God doesn't ordain (or design) the time and manner of the worst parts of life and death, we are then left to wonder whether He is unable to alter them to something more favorable, or is for whatever reason unwilling to exercise his infinite ability to do so, despite being unhappy about the circumstance. Both of those are greatly troubling, hardly comforting ideas.

In my experience with Alice, coming to grips with God's relationship to her cancer was emotionally and theologically difficult. Actual truth is obnoxiously unchanging. I've discovered that certain things I thought I knew weren't actually true. I try to think of it this way: Truth can't be destroyed, but things we think are true but aren't can be destroyed, and sometimes experience is a like a wrecking ball that assaults us and helps us quickly sort out what really *is* true and what we only *thought* was true. The resultant pile of rubble is our shattered delusions. Hurts sometimes, but it's good in the end. Living in a delusion may be fun for a while, but it's best just to know what's really true.

Perhaps, someone might suggest, God was as surprised by this as we were. Fair enough; I understand the desire to approach it that way. But if that were the case, He'd naturally be quite willing and eager to fix it, especially if the right pressure, we might say, was applied in the right way. Since He didn't fix it, despite all the pressure applied, one might be left with the feeling that nobody is really at the controls of the world. If God is like Mr. Incredible, just out there trying to clean up the mess, in Alice's case, He must have failed. If God doesn't see tragedies coming, they must necessarily be random and at root, meaningless. The death of Alice would be, it seems to me, the result of someone responsible for fixing the problem asleep at the helm.

Perhaps God *allowed* this thing. He wasn't a huge fan of the idea, maybe it wasn't his first choice, but he decided not to fix it, to let it happen anyway. I truly believe that since God created natural law, he seems rather hesitant to violate it. He can make a rock issue a river of water, an axe head float, or dead men come stumbling out of their own grave, but those are historical exceptions, not the rule.

Speaking of God *allowing* a thing leaves a little taste in my mouth that says, "This isn't the *best*, but maybe God can salvage a piece of it and get some use out of it." On the front end of a tragedy, thinking about God in this way lets us maintain the notion that God wouldn't actively cause us pain, only passively let it happen. But on the back side of it, we're left to wrestle with a God who doesn't *want* bad things to happen to us but doesn't *fix* them when they do, and that seems almost nonsensical. After all, it takes more effort for me to press the spacebar as I'm typing this than it would for God to have healed Alice's DIPG.

He didn't say "no" because He's too lazy. There must be more to it than this.

So I finally landed squarely where I really began in my thinking before this ordeal began: God ordains even tragedies like this. It was part of His plan from the beginning. But in those early days following diagnosis as I held Alice tightly and wept, my notions of what God is like were shaken, and shaken deeply. What kind of God loves Alice and me with infinite love, possesses infinite foresight and power, but builds this kind of pain and sorrow into our lives?

I spent time with Job, rolling his words around in my head, "The Lord gives, and *the Lord* takes away." But it wasn't *God* that killed Job's kids. *Satan* whipped up that windstorm. Still, Job said it was the Lord who took away. Job said many things to God but spoke not a word to Satan. Luther is credited with saying that there is a devil, and he's God's devil. Better to talk to the carpenter than his hammer.

Which brings me back to prayer. If God has ordained these things to happen, why pray about *anything*? That's a meaningful question. It's problematic. If the end and the beginning are set in the Divine Mind and the world is going to unfold as designed, why pray? One of the best answers, though not entirely satisfactory, is that since God's plan is perfect, prayer changes *me*, bringing my imperfect heart into agreement with God's perfect program. God's program doesn't need changing, *I* do.

That's getting there. But that's by no means the whole story.

God's Promises

The Bible contains numerous, explicit promises that God not only hears, but absolutely *will* answer the prayers of His children. Here are a couple of them:

"...whatever you ask in prayer, you will receive, if you have faith." (Matt 21:22)

"Whatever you ask in my name, this I will do, that the Father may be glorified in the Son." (John 14:13)

"If you abide in me, and my words abide in you, ask whatever you wish, and it will be done for you." (John 15:7. Also see John 15:16 and 16:23 for the same sentiment, meaning Jesus repeated this promise no less than four times in the "Farewell Discourse!")

"Beloved, if our heart does not condemn us, we have confidence before God; and whatever we ask we receive from him, because we keep his commandments and do what pleases him." (1 John 3:21-22)

I take these verses to mean a couple of important things:

First, God promises to give his people what they ask for. Prayer is more than asking for stuff, but let's face it – the prayers we pray are usually heavily skewed to presenting to God a list of things we want, often things we can't directly provide for ourselves – wisdom to make decisions when we can't know all the variables, protection from hostile forces beyond our control, or curing Alice of her DIPG. Jesus flat out said "ask…" so it's not improper.

Second, it seems self-evident from these texts that God will do things when people pray that He would not do if they didn't. He could have said, "Ask, and if what you desire is already part of My plan, you'll get it." Or he could have said, "Ask, and if you don't get what you want, at least *you'll* be changed, even if the situation isn't." Jesus was of necessity cryptic at times, but this doesn't seem to be one of those times.

I doubt I am the only person who has ever worked through the Wednesday prayer meeting list of people with infirmities that needed to be fixed, journeys that needed mercies, or that thing about "watchcare," remaining completely confident in God's ability to supernaturally intervene in every case but rather certain that the outcome would be just about the same whether I prayed or not. Let us be perfectly blunt: Christian kids will probably get over the flu same as their heathen neighbors, a Christian family's vacation to the beach will likely be made as safely (or not) as a non-Christian's. Great-grandma Agnes down at the nursing home is probably not moving back to the farm, no matter how much I might pray she would.

As we prayed for Alice to be healed by the hand of God, sometimes the thought ran through my mind, or was vocalized by someone, that if she died, our prayers would be answered because she would be fully and finally healed. But this was not at all satisfactory to me. We prayed because we *didn't* want Alice to die. If dying and being healed in heaven was what we wanted, we could have just not prayed, God wouldn't have any prayers to answer, and she would very naturally die and be ultimately healed in heaven. To me, the notion that Alice being healed in that sense was an affirmative answer to our prayers was like praying at midnight for a ray of sunshine, then claiming answered prayer when the sun rises the next morning – does that really count?

The Caveats

I must say a word here, because it needs to be said. The promises God gave us concerning prayer are usually closely accompanied by an "if." *If* you abide in me, ask what you want. James says *if* you ask doubting, you won't get what you're looking for. Peter indicates that inconsiderate husbands offer up ineffectual prayers. The Lord will give us the desires of our heart... *if* we delight ourselves in Him. And very basic but also worth remembering, we must ask *in Jesus' name*; answered prayers are distinctly *Christian* prayers.

It's almost possible to get God entirely off the hook for answering our prayers by subjecting his mighty promises to the death of a thousand qualifications. There's just enough fine print surrounding them that perhaps expecting God to answer our prayers is the rough equivalent of expecting Facebook to fulfill its promise to value our privacy – it sounds great on the face of it, but break out a magnifying glass and study the tiny words long enough and you'll realize it was never intended to . happen.

I'm not going to try to work through the caveats concerning prayer, only to say they are very much real, and very much needed. If

God was nothing more than genie in a black leather-bound bottle (to grossly mix metaphors) granting every short-sighted, somewhat selfish request (which probably describes an embarrassingly large percentage of our requests), we would live in a chaotic and conflicted world driven along, not by the perfect purposes of God, but by the conflicting whims of people steering God according to their own desires. I must say, however, the now-extinct Wednesday evening prayer service would experience quite a resurrection if prayer yielded an immediately higher, more tangible return on investment.

Among the thousands of people praying for Alice, I firmly believe someone somewhere must have done it in accordance with Jesus' promises. Maybe it wasn't me, but somewhere there must have been a decent husband delighting himself in the Lord praying in obedience to the prompting of the Spirit, begging God to heal Alice. Somewhere a godly woman exercised tremendous faith, never doubting God's love or His ability to cure what no medical professional now knows how to cure. Alice was prayed for by an unusually large number of Pastors, men whose very life's work, their calling from God is encapsulated by two words in Acts 6, one of which is "prayer." Godly women passionately prayed for Alice; innocent young children exercised their pure and simple faith on her behalf.

If God makes such wonderful sounding promises that He will hear and answer our prayers, and if thousands of people take Him at His word and pray, then why didn't we get what we wanted? The caveats are real, but surely someone must have met them and broke through.

The Root of the Matter

This brings me to the root of the matter, the heart of our prayers for Alice.

"Father, heal Alice!" That was our prayer. Why did we ask that? Of all the prayers we could have offered, why that one? And did you notice that we organically and almost universally prayed the exact same prayer? I didn't run into anyone that told me they were praying that Alice's hair would turn blonde or that she would be able to run faster or lift heavier objects. No, we prayed that the cancer would be taken away, that she would survive.

At the heart of the matter, we prayed for Alice's *happiness*. Suffering under a brain tumor is scary, it's potentially painful, it's inconvenient, and whatever we may call it, it isn't fun and it doesn't create happiness. Sure, we admired her for her happiness *in spite of* the cancer, but that's another matter altogether. Cancer was a drag on her happiness. We didn't want her happiness burdened. We wanted it unthreatened and free. We wanted her to be happier free from cancer than the happiness she experienced in spite of it.

For that matter, we prayed for Alice's healing because *we* wanted to be happy. We didn't want to go through the sadness of losing her. We have a burning desire to be happy, and Alice's tumor threatened her happiness and therefore ours. And we were sad, weren't we? We are sad, even still. We didn't want to be sad, or to miss out on the happiness she brought to us.

"Ah!" someone will say, "she *is* happy. Our prayers are answered!" I still don't think that counts. After all, not only did we believe she would be happy if she died, we actually believed she would be *happier* in heaven. But we prayed anyway, because it seemed like the right thing to do. We prayed because we wanted God to make her life and ours happier. We prayed because we wanted God to make her life better, and we really believed that by praying God would hear us and improve her life and ours.

To the ones who will insist in a conversation such as this that we ought to pursue a joy that transcends happiness, unhitched from circumstances, or that we can be simultaneously unhappy and joyful, I hear what you're saying, but I'm not totally there yet. Proper distinctions I love and cherish; unnecessary ones seem to me to be covering something up. There are reasons for both why we prayed for her happiness by appealing to God to alter the circumstance and why we marveled at her happiness *in spite of* the circumstances. It seems to me however that heaven will not contain unpleasant circumstances whereby we may authenticate our joy by being simultaneously unhappy and joyful.

Changing the Way We Prayed the Same Thing

After radiation, we rejoiced that Alice's tumor had disappeared. We wondered whether God had heard our prayers and answered them just like we asked. It seemed a thin hope, but it was hopeful. Cancer was gone; perhaps it wouldn't come back?

Then it did come back. And when it came back, with a particularly aggressive vengeance, I noticed a shift in the way I prayed and the way others prayed. This wasn't orchestrated, it just happened. We began to pray not so much that God would heal her, though we still did, but primarily that He would take her gently. It's a strange thing to beg God to heal your child one week and beg Him to take her away the next. But really, it was the same prayer. It was a prayer that God would hear us and improve her happiness (and ours). Maybe God would hear our prayers and have mercy on her and she really would lie down to sleep and never wake up. That didn't seem so bad.

So we changed the way we prayed the same thing: Father, improve Alice's lot; give her increased happiness, even in death.

Truth be told, I'm not sure that prayer was answered, certainly not like I wanted it to be. The days leading up to June 8 contain some of the darkest hours of my life, moments in which I felt abandoned or even betrayed by God. I begged Him to take her, to spare her from the agony she was going through, and he didn't do it. Increase her happiness, Lord!

Changing Us

Praying for Alice changed me, and perhaps it has changed others who prayed. I found that wrestling with God taught me a great many things about God that I didn't know and a great many things about myself that I didn't like. I learned early on to trust that God's plan was the best, I learned how difficult but ultimately sweet it is to know that the hardest things in life are "momentary" and "light," but they produce a glory that is "eternal" and "weighty." I learned that God is far more willing than I had imagined for His children, even the smallest and weakest of them, to endure intense suffering. And I came to really believe that one day it will be worth it all, that looking back we will feel incredibly grateful that God planned this journey in exactly this way.

Through this process, I hope I've become a better Dad and a more faithful Christian, that I will have developed a greater appreciation for God's wisdom, a deeper hatred for my own sin, an increased affection for the life awaiting me on the other side of my own grave, and a wiser approach to life on this side. I've learned to better integrate the God who resided so well in my private, religious life where He lived in the relative safety and obscurity of abstract thought into the affairs of public, daily, ordinary life.

We have been challenged to learn to trust in the goodness of a God who doesn't do what we would do if we were him. We have been challenged to really believe in heaven, and not just because we wanted happy thoughts, but because we really want to know where Alice is so we can go see her again. I miss her and want to hold her again. Really badly. Like David, I say she can't come to me, but I will go to her!

But this is not entirely satisfactory either. While our prayers did include our own desire to avoid being sad, we weren't primarily praying for ourselves. We weren't praying that we would grow in faith, or grow in holiness. We weren't praying that our vision of God would be expanded. These things were pleasant side-effects, but we were praying for Alice, after all. We were praying that her lot would be improved, that our prayers would result in her happiness.

It seemed to me then if I were to stop at this point in my thinking, despite all these good things, God's promises remain unfulfilled; we really didn't get what we asked for yet.

Changing Alice

I titled this *The Vault of Unanswered Prayers*. "Put my tears in a bottle," David said. Don't forget that I cried them, Lord. Don't forget that we prayed these prayers Lord, prayers you promised to answer, but didn't.

When I was a little boy in Sunday School, I was taught that God gave one of three answers to every prayer: Yes, No, or Later. "Yes" is what we want, and "Later" is a delayed yes or a temporary no, sort of a compromise position. But I don't recall Jesus saying God would tell us "no." Quite the contrary. At best, it seems to me that "No" isn't an answer so much as an aborted, ineffectual prayer that dies on one of the necessary caveats attending God's promises.

There are two famous New Testament cases where God apparently said "no" to good and proper prayer. One was Jesus in the garden – "if it is possible, remove this cup from Me." The other was the Apostle Paul – "Take away this thorn in my flesh!" Both of these were prayers for increased happiness (through, I might add, altering difficult and painful circumstances). Jesus' cross was torturously painful, not to mention humiliating. Paul's thorn made life and ministry much harder than it would have been without it. The pain was a drag on their desired happiness.

Jesus prayed, "Not my will, yours be done." That could mean Jesus is just saying the Father is the boss, and he'll sigh and accept the verdict. But it could also mean that Jesus trusted that the Father really did want Him to be happy, and his path to greatest happiness was *through*, not around, the greatest pain. After all, on the other side of the cross, Jesus received an increased eternal glory he would not have possessed apart from the suffering he endured. He prayed for happiness in a temporal sense ("no cross, please!"), God gave it to him in an eternal sense ("I will make you King of kings!").

Paul only asked three times to have his problem fixed. Shoot, I prayed a hundred times for Alice's deal. But God told Paul that his thorn, his pain, the drag on his happiness, spared him spiritual shipwreck – if not for that thorn, he would have become an egomaniacal headcase and ruined his ministry. With the thorn, he finished his life saying, "There is laid up for me a crown of righteousness…" He prayed for temporal happiness and was rewarded with an increased eternal happiness he would not have otherwise had.

So here is how I understand our prayers for Alice finally answered: we prayed for her increased happiness, we desired that God give her an improvement in her circumstances that she would not have received if we didn't pray. And as we prayed, God used her cancer and our utter helplessness to draw us to Himself and draw us to each other; she became a tool in God's hands to make some people better Christians, and perhaps to make some people Christians in the first place. These are things that would not have happened if Alice didn't get DIPG, they wouldn't have happened if she was immediately healed, and they wouldn't have happened if we hadn't wrestled with God in prayer first for her healing then for her death, and finally coming to the difficult but inescapable conclusion that this is the path of greatest happiness for her.

My conclusion: her happiness is increased because of how much she did for us as she walked that difficult and deadly path.

Heaven will be eternally sweeter for Alice because we prayed for her improved happiness, and in our praying for Alice God did mighty things in our hearts and lives. She has been used by God to do things in our own lives that will improve our lives for all eternity, and it would be improper for God not to eternally reward her for her part. We prayed, Alice's happiness waned. We prayed again, wrestling to gain a bigger understanding of God, and Alice died. And we wrestled again, our faith growing (sometimes properly shrinking) and our hearts becoming increasingly disillusioned with this fallen world and anxious to experience the perfection of the next. Alice in some sense brought heaven nearer to us and made God clearer to us. Until we wrestled with the difficult and seemingly unpleasant aspects of who God is, we couldn't really appreciate the glorious, gracious aspects of who He is either. And when all is said and done, Alice will be honored as God's chosen servant to turn our hearts in profoundly deep and sweet childlike trust to the wisdom of the God who doesn't always do as we wish, but always what is best. As I understand it, that means heaven will be sweeter, richer, happier for Alice than if we never bothered to pray, never bothered to wrestle with God through these hard things, never allowed God the chance to stretch and grow us as we plead, with apparent futility it seemed, for Alice's happiness.

The vault of unanswered prayers for Alice's increased happiness will be emptied and gloriously answered, just as promised. Every prayer we offered up on her behalf will be fully, gladly, and eternally answered by our doting, all wise, magnificently generous Father who will escalate her happiness into realms we, and she, never could have imagined. Is this just the pipe dreams of a Dad who doesn't want his friends to feel like they wasted their time and effort praying for his daughter, doesn't want her life to be considered incomplete or less than significant, or her untimely death to have been an avoidable, unfortunate mistake? God will be the judge of that. But I don't think so. I hope it's an expression of a faith that He kindly used our very own Alice to form in me.

Chapter 24

Missing

*On the seventh day the child died... David said to his servants,
"Is the child dead?" They said, "He is dead." Then David
arose from the earth and washed and anointed himself and
changed his clothes. And he went into the house of the Lord
and worshiped. He then went to his own house. And when he
asked, they set food before him, and he ate. 2 Sam. 12:19b-20*

Sept. 9, 2018

The record of King David losing his infant son was never too far from my mind during Alice's final weeks. The passionate prayers and sorrows before death, followed by a seemingly immediate return to "normal" life sort of laid out a simple pattern for me that I hoped to follow.

The night Alice died, after I'd lifted her lifeless, already stiffening body off our bed, carried her through the kitchen, out the front door, and set her in the back of that shiny black minivan, laid her on a cot that was far too big for her little body, kissed her cool forehead one last time, pulled up the zipper of that adult size bag – after all, this ride wasn't designed for kids – I walked back into the house where my Dad was seated at the table, and with reference to David that I knew he'd understand, I said to him, "Time to take a shower and eat something."

As I write this paragraph, we are now two and a half months along in our journey without Alice. And while our road still has hills and valleys, twists and turns, and we hit various (sometimes unseen) bumps and potholes, it is beginning to slowly smooth and straighten out. Describing life as we're now experiencing it is kind of like painting a still portrait of an action scene, trying to take something in motion and freeze it. As soon as I write this, we'll probably feel a little different and I'll wish I'd waited longer to be able to give a better, fuller, clearer picture.

Drinking the Cup

In the first days and weeks following Alice's death, the best way to describe how we felt was that we were drinking a cocktail of all kinds of conflicting emotions, and each one seemed to have various moments in the forefront of our minds. In the first days we felt sad, of course, but also a sense of relief, mostly for Alice, because some of her final days were, to be honest, brutal, and we didn't want her to have to endure any more of them. The peaceful rest of death seemed preferable to the torture of cancer or the partial relief she got through morphine and the anti-anxiety drugs we had to administer.

Speaking of which, I think perhaps one of the hardest things I've ever had to do, and a job I hated so badly I couldn't let anyone else do it, was to fill little plastic syringes with drugs every couple of hours and squirt them inside her cheek, essentially putting and keeping her in a drug-induced stupor. I hated it only slightly less than watching her semi-conscious agitation and fear as she struggled and gasped for one gargly breath after another, for hours that seemed like weeks. So there was a relief when that was over. A relief for her, and frankly, even with a sense of guilt for feeling it, relief for us.

We had the luxury (and I hope you'll understand my use of the term "luxury") of having, from about day 4 in Alice's journey, way back in September of last year, relative certainty of its outcome. Wanting to be as realistic as possible about this thing meant that we had to take seriously the 0% survival statistic that accompanies DIPG. I often think if she had 50% odds, or 80% odds, in the end we'd have felt an exponentially greater sense of disappointment, a sense of guilt for being too slow to discover and diagnose the thing, for pursuing the wrong treatment, or for any number of other possible regrets when she died. On top of all the other feelings, we'd have felt like we failure Alice. But the seeming certainty of death (tempered, to be sure, with a cautious hope) meant that for 8-1/2 months we had more or less been preparing for this day, and when it came, we weren't surprised, and though sad the journey was over, it was nice to finally be out from under the shadow of impending doom, the fear of what that day would be like, and rather than wonder in fear what it would be like, actually face the thing itself.

Back around February when Alice was feeling really good, she spent a night at my brother's house, having a sleepover with her cousin Claire. She was excited to go and not surprisingly had a wonderful time. I remember when we sat down as a family for supper that night, as we usually do, and her spot on the bench was empty. It was kind of an eerie feeling, like "this is how it's going to be someday." It doesn't really matter whose seat is empty at the dinner table, even with the other seven filled it just doesn't feel right; it's too quiet.

It's always been amazing to me that whenever a new baby is added to the family, in a matter of days it seems impossible to imagine a time when that little person wasn't there. We only had 6 children for 9 months, but after Violet was born, it felt like we never had less.

When Alice died, we quickly discovered that subtraction doesn't work as fast as addition. Having eight stuffed into our seven-passenger van felt so right and normal that when Alice wasn't there anymore and everyone had their own seat, it seemed like riding in a cargo plane – big and empty. Something much bigger than a four-year-old seemed to be missing.

If addition quickly feels like someone's always been there, subtraction, when it does finally and slowly begin to set in, feels sometimes like she was never there in the first place. And that's a different kind of lousy feeling. Alice left all kinds of tracks in our hearts and around our world. The pictures she drew on the living room window are still there, we filled up a chest of the toys that she loved the most, and her bed is still full of her stuffed animals. I saved her wristbands from her hospital visits and use them as bookmarks.

But her tracks are fading, slowly. Her towel doesn't hang in the shower anymore, her shoes aren't scattered around the front door. The sound of SpongeBob's annoying voice or "The Funny Guys" hitting each other isn't the near constant background noise of our house any longer. The bag of pretzels she wanted and left half eaten (the bag left open in the drawer long enough that nobody wanted to finish them) has finally been thrown away. "Eggs like a ball" aren't in high demand around here anymore; they were kind of her thing. Her clothes have all been washed and put away, out of sight and slowly out of mind.

Michele perhaps expressed the feeling best when she wrote this: *I wish I could go back to life before cancer desecrated her little body. I hate all that it did to her! It paralyzed her, it took away her dignity, it reduced her to a mere shadow of the girl we loved and God allowed it, maybe He even planned it, and I have to figure out how I can be okay with that. I am not at all sure how to get there from here... I want to cling to the past because it has my Alice in it – the real Alice and I feel like if I stop hurting, and talking about her life, and missing her it will be like she never existed, and I can't bear that. I feel as though if I could just keep the memories of her laughter and her funny sayings and words and her fancy dresses and all of her Aliceness fresh and bright in my mind then she can't really be gone from me. They start to fade anyways in spite of all attempts, as time marches on and there is nothing left to do but accept the unacceptable and try to keep moving forward in life. Sadly, forward is further away from her and so I very much hesitate to go in that direction. I just want to sit here; a reminiscing stick-in-the-mud willfully caught in a time warp.*

One of the things that Michele and I often did together in those first days and weeks in order to kind of recalibrate our memories was to look through pictures, remembering her smiles and laughs. We have pictures from her last week or so, but we rarely look at them. We don't mind so much remembering the bad stuff, and we're not keen about forgetting anything, it's just that we'd prefer our "default" memories to be happy ones, not sad ones.

Speaking of pictures, something I never really anticipated is the odd joy of seeing a picture of her I'd never seen before. Once in a while, the kids or a friend or relative will show us one from their phone we've never seen before, and I love that. It's like the happiness of watching a deleted scene at the end of your favorite movie... you know how the story goes, how it ends, and that doesn't change, but seeing a new piece of that story gives a freshness to the familiar. In some sense, new pictures are like having a new day with her.

The Big and the Small

I think I was in Pastor Bob's office doing some planning for Alice's funeral, and as we talked about the size of crowd we might expect to attend, he said to me, "Alice was larger than life." For almost nine months, we lived with this little girl who, quite unknown to her (or as far as she did know, she hid it well) brought us into a world filled with big things.

Her tumor was big, the threat it posed to her was big. The response of family, friends, and strangers was massive. Her benefit on that wonderful December evening still amazes me for its size and scope. The gifts of kindness and love that came from across the community and even the nation were colossal. Alice T-Shirts, Alice Facebook profile pictures, and my Aunt Lori's red "Pray for Alice" bracelets, one of which is still on my left wrist, were everywhere. Her funeral was huge.

We lived in this world of big things. We traveled to Florida courtesy of Make-A-Wish. We spent time at the Wisconsin Dells. My brothers remodeled half the main level on our house to make life better for her. We were given lots of attention almost everywhere we went; strangers knew our names and people still unknown to us picked up our check at restaurants. We experienced "once in a lifetime" kinds of things quite frequently. We ate like kings courtesy of some dear people who stuffed our freezer with "sticks," bacon, and anything else Alice loved.

By sheer necessity, we pushed aside so many mundane things that are significant enough in the normal flow of life because we lived primarily preoccupied with the specter of life and death on the front burner of our minds. And all that activity and the unique and special things were good and right, and a wonderful community of friends and family came together and gave so much for Alice to have the best final months a little girl could have. And she did. You never knew a happier kid, notwithstanding all she endured. And we're thankful for what you gave her.

But now we're trying to readjust to the small things. It's hard to care about changing the oil on the van when your daughter may only have two weeks to live, or return a phone call or email when we have just laid her in the ground. The big thing pushed the little things aside. But immediately after the big thing was gone, the little ones still felt ridiculously insignificant if not downright silly and a waste of time. Problem is, the little things are what we had left; they are normal life. And without the big thing, not caring about the little things kind of meant there was nothing left to care about. That's an empty, frustrating feeling. Our purpose in life was, for almost a year, to care for Alice. Then she was gone. And the normal responsibilities of life just seemed so, well, meaningless.

That's changing. Slowly.

Several weeks ago Michele and I went to visit our friend Linda down at Braham Monument to order Alice's gravestone. That was harder than I anticipated, probably because it felt like the final thing on our "to-do" list for Alice. It's strange to not have any more to do for her. Our parental work on her behalf is done. We wish it wasn't.

This week Alice's gravestone showed up. I walked out to the cemetery and stared at that piece of black granite carved with her name, two dates, and Michele's drawing of Alice walking with Aslan. Inscribed across the bottom are the words "The Lord is My Shepherd..." I sat down on the grass in front of it and shed a few tears. It's almost ironic – this cold, hard block of granite designed to withstand the elements of this harsh world for a century or more casting its shadow over the resting place of my warm, tender-hearted little girl who wasn't able to survive them for five years.

Since some have asked, here's a few words on grieving, from my perspective anyway. A week or so ago I read C.S. Lewis' *A Grief Observed*, in which he describes the days and weeks following the death of his wife, and I commend it to you as a brief, but incredibly insightful look into the mind of a man in sorrow, communicated in a way only Lewis could.

Until the past several months, I've thought of "grieving" as synonymous with "being sad." But, as any rank amateur in the grieving business probably knows, it's deeper and more complicated than that. While I've felt sad, the reality is I haven't felt as sad as often or as deeply I expected. It feels good to feel sad, and even to cry. I recently joked to Michele that crying for me is like sneezing for her – I feel it coming, screw up my face, close my eyes, take a deep breath, and prepare for launch, but halfway through the mission aborts, and that's that.

Grieving is adjusting to a life that is permanently diminished (in a "this life" sense...) It's coming to terms with a new, unpleasant reality. For us, it's a reality that doesn't have Alice in it. And having tasted a world in which we loved her and she loved us, it's hard to enjoy this new version of the life where something we treasured so dearly is no longer here. Something unique, irreplaceable, and infinitely valuable has been lost, and let's just say the thing as it is... the old reality was better than the new one; I don't like this one as much.

That's probably why, when a person dies, we stand around and talk about how we'll see that person again – we've experienced a better kind of world, where the departed was with us, and we want to return to it. If all the pieces aren't in the box, it's just not a very satisfying puzzle anymore. I understand better the shepherd who leaves the ninety-nine to get the one that's gone missing. Grief is going back to the ninety-nine empty handed, trying to figure out why you'd happily trade them all away just to get the one back.

Of course, Christian grief has something very distinct about it: Christian grief lives in full view of the reality of death and fully recognizes how hard it is to go from a better reality with Alice in it to a worse one where her little body lies beneath the grass. And it lives in view of the reality that for us, we may have to die ourselves before we see her again. Still, hope is not lost. There remains a grave from which the Occupant exited the premises under His own power 1,990 years ago, with the promise that He'd return and empty the graves of all His family, which we are by faith. Our hope is in the risen Jesus. We have none other. All other hopes let us down. Radiation, chemo, even *gasp* natural foods and supplements. The only hope that remains is a hope in One who can reverse even death itself. So we grieve, but with hope.

Smaller Faith

Recently I was working my way through 1 Peter 1 where Peter writes about our faith being tested in suffering like gold being purified by fire. The picture is simple enough: heat the gold up so hot it melts, and all the not-gold separates from the is-gold or gets burnt up. This simple, if violent process makes the gold pure and therefore better and more valuable. It also means the original lump of gold is smaller.

I hope you'll understand what I mean when I say I have a smaller faith. Faith is, in simple terms, what we expect God to do in given circumstances. Thing is, God is who He is, and my expectations don't make Him what He is. Turns out He's more interested in being Himself than meeting my expectations.

From the beginning of this ordeal, as I've said repeatedly, I really expected it to end like it did. I hoped it wouldn't, prayed it wouldn't, and all that, but I have two eyes and can read medical reports – little kids die from DIPG. God lets it happen. Little kids die from all kinds of things. Today Michele counted at least thirteen other children in the little cemetery where Alice is laid to rest.

So that wasn't a surprise. But what was a surprise was how difficult those last days were for Alice. When I wrote at the time "in the end, she died peacefully," there's a lot hidden by the little words "in the end…" Just before the end my faith was run through a fire, and some of it got burned off.

I kind of thought along these lines: "Here I am, Lord, your servant, and all I have is ultimately yours. Even my children. If you want to take our Alice from us, she is Yours. I don't really like it, I'd rather keep her, but you are God and I'm not; take her if you like." What I expected in return was for God to respect my submission and make the process as easy and painless as possible – especially for Alice. But it wasn't as easy and painless as possible. Parts of it were torture, for her to endure, and for me to watch. I felt disappointed by God – here I'd done everything to try to honor him and his sovereignty over all things, and in return it seemed fair to expect that he'd make this as soft and tender an exit as possible.

Turns out God and I weren't partners in this thing. He called all the shots. It's not even like He would call three shots and then give me the fourth. He got them *all*. My contract of faith included this clause that read something like, "Before it gets too bad, God is going to show up and make it easy to endure. He's going to sweep in and blanket our souls with sweetness and hope, and we'll feel a closeness and comfort we've never felt before and look back on this experience with a kind of sacred nostalgia." Seemed reasonable enough. I've heard other people express their experience that way.

For us, that's not the way it went down. Almost like Jacob, I had to wrestle for two days with a God who would not only take my Alice away, but in the process let her endure some really difficult, and to my way of thinking at the time, entirely unnecessary trauma before he took her. And when I looked for Him in those darkest moments my soul has ever endured, He seemed nowhere to be found. I called out and didn't hear His voice. That is not to say, of course, that He wasn't there. He just wasn't there in the way I expected Him to be. I give you permission to read that as me being disappointed in God; however, my disappointment is a reflection of my expectations, not some failure on God's part. He kept all His promises. Every one of them. He just hadn't made certain promises I thought He had.

As I write these final thoughts late on a Saturday night, finishing up what I began a couple weeks ago, it's three months to the hour that I carried Alice out of the house for the last time. I'm here to say God is faithful. He is good. He has not let us down. The suffering was more intense than I ever imagined or could have prepared myself for, and believe me, I tried to prepare myself for it. When He put my faith through the fire, it hurt. It's supposed to hurt, that's how you know it's doing something. Part of this new reality I'm adjusting to is a reality in which I have different expectations of God. And I don't mean that in a bad way. I trust Him, more than ever. And I really want to know Him as He really is. And I do, more truly than ever.

Following the sudden, violent death of his ten children Job said, "Though he slay me, yet will I trust him." That's a great line that sounds so fun to try out on one's own lips until God doesn't step in and eradicate a daughter's brain cancer. Then it becomes a dogged determination that says, "I have no idea why God would do this, but He doesn't require my permission or owe me an explanation." Don't get me wrong, I'd love an explanation. But He's God and I'm not. He's working all things together for eternal good; I'm just begging for life on this side of death to be good, since that's (unfortunately) usually as far ahead as I look.

I also noticed in my reading of Job that his initial reaction of wonderful trust was not long afterwards followed by a tumultuous period of despair, complaint, and even rather impolitely demanding answers from God. I'm rather certain I didn't do any better, and hopefully not much worse, than he did.

Whether or not I like how God works in the moment is irrelevant. And somehow, on this side of the darkest hour of my life, that's strangely comforting. It's good to have a loving God who maps out our lives: the good, the bad, and the insanely painful, as though death itself is hardly worth considering since for Him, it's so easily overcome.

Well, like the stone is the period on Alice's earthly life, this chapter will mark the period of my telling her story. Lewis repeatedly complained in *A Grief Observed* that he fell into talking about himself rather than his beloved, and in this post, I feel the same disappointment in myself.

As a family, we're "starting over." The immediate days following Alice's departure and funeral we were still kind of energized by the significance of the event and its attendant activities, so we went about the business of getting back into some semblance of normalcy. After a couple weeks, we ran out of gas physically and emotionally and were ready for a break. So we spent a week on a houseboat up on Namakan Lake, just being together and making some memories, our first pleasant memories in the post-Alice era. Hard, but necessary, and ultimately really good.

My heart, slowly returning to life, remains full of gratitude for all the kindnesses we have received and continue to receive, and I am often amazed and incredibly happy at the impact of Alice's story in the hearts and lives of you who have let her in, even though it meant you would be crushed along with us. Join us in eternal hope. As Michele and I say to each other during the dark moments, "It's going to be okay."

PS. Whenever I finish one of these, I always end up wishing I'd said this or that or thanked this person or that one. This being the final chapter, and for whatever reason the most difficult to write (not necessarily emotionally difficult, but somehow just thinking coherent thoughts and stringing them together is still obnoxiously hard to do), that feeling is particularly strong right now. But I've already made this far too long and included far too little. Still, I wish to extend our deepest gratitude to all of you who have faithfully walked this journey with us, sometimes at great expense, and still do.

Chapter 25

How Alice Entered Wonderland

or

What Happens to Kids Who Die?

And they were bringing children to him that he might touch them, and the disciples rebuked them. But when Jesus saw it, he was indignant and said to them, "Let the children come to me; do not hinder them, for to such belongs the kingdom of God. Truly, I say to you, whoever does not receive the kingdom of God like a child shall not enter it." Mark 10:13-15

December 15, 2018

I wasn't sure I'd ever get this written, but it really is the only additional thing I wanted to write concerning Alice, so after a few attempts, here goes…

I believe Alice is in the Palace, or if you like, she is truly Alice in Wonderland. What I want to do is attempt to explain *why* I think she's there. And in doing so, I want to be an encouragement to the many other parents who have lost little ones. One thing this ordeal has taught us: we are not alone in our sorrow. If I have wondered about Alice's whereabouts, perhaps others have too. Hopefully this helps; it's helped me. At Christmastime, we need something to be cheerful about, because there seems to be more tears than smiles in our house this year…

RC Sproul tells the story of the young monk Martin Luther taking a trip to Rome. While there, he climbed "the holy stairs," supposedly the same stairs Jesus climbed as he stood before Pilate, later hauled off to Rome. As Luther ascended, he stopped on each step, kissing it and saying prayers, in the hope of relieving his grandparents' suffering in purgatory. As RC tells it, he reached the top step, said his final prayer, and then muttered to himself, *"But what if it isn't true?"* Really, does kissing stairs and saying prayers get grandparents out of purgatory? For a whole host of reasons, including serious doubts concerning the existence of purgatory and the wisdom of smooching steps, I don't think it does.

It's all well and good to envision my Alice laughing and carrying on and having a jolly old time in heaven; I even prefer to think she's joined a chorus of impatient saints (Rev. 6:9-11) urging Jesus to hurry along and wrap up earthly history so she can get her body back, her family back, and get on with being a kid again. Spirits don't eat noodles or "eggs like a ball;" I can't help but wonder if she doesn't miss them from time to time, and in her obsessive way repeat, "Jesus, we can have some *later*," which really means, "I'll give you two minutes, then I'm asking again…"

Imagination is all well and good, to a point. But a thing isn't true because I want it to be. What Alice is doing right now has little to do with my imagination; it has everything to with a reality I can't see. On top of that, I'm a total cynic concerning those who claim to have gone to heaven and come back. That's another matter for another day. At any rate, if my imagination determined reality, she'd be bodily sitting here beside me right now playing with her little toys. So that doesn't work.

I read recently that half or even up to three quarters of all pregnancies end in the death of the child before the mother is even aware that she's pregnant. Of course, others miscarry after they are aware. That means that up to 75% of the population of heaven or hell will be comprised of persons who never took a breath, said a single word, or even experienced a moment of consciousness. If you add the number of children killed by cancer, SIDS, or abortion, that percentage goes up even higher. This is a big deal.

Scripture seems to indicate that the same body that dies is the same one that's eventually perfected and raised. I take that to mean in whatever state of development it's in, that's the state it continues post-resurrection, all fixed up. A 95 year-old made perfectly healthy is a youthfully energetic, fully mature human being eternally at the pinnacle of vivacity. When Alice's little body is raised, she's still going to be a 4 year old child with lots of growing to do. That's what I think, anyway. I don't exactly know how that translates into Alice's 4 siblings that reached heaven before her via miscarriage and how their development will happen. But I really do believe that Shelly and I will somehow get to raise those little ones too. If you tied me to a stake and threatened to burn me if I didn't recant that belief, I'd recant. But if you only gave me a paper cut and poured lemon juice in it, I'd stick to my guns and defend it!

For several years and long predating Alice's cancer, some of my dearest and godliest friends and I have had this ongoing debate about the destiny of children who die, and some have tenaciously held that: a) some kids make it to heaven, b) some kids don't, and c) we just can't know which ones. They have good company in the history of theology, probably more and better company than me. I've always maintained they all make it. That makes for some interesting (and delicate!) conversations between us now.

It's one thing to argue logical points over a cup of coffee with friends, but it would be another thing for them to accompany me to Alice's grave and say, "I sure wish we knew where she was right now." None of my friends has ever done that, and I doubt they would, and I'd never put them in that position. *No one* that I know could or would say to me out loud, "I'm so sorry that Alice is now frying in hell." There's a pretty strong consensus that she's in the company of angels. But to me, that only makes the question *"What if it isn't true?"* all the more challenging.

It's admittedly difficult to think through the subject with any sort of objectivity. Everyone I know of or have read, even those who believe in the damnation of certain little ones on pretty solid theological grounds seem to *prefer* they all be saved. There's actually something to that, and we shouldn't ignore the significance of that universal, instinctive desire. I'm comfortable with and even happy about Stalin and Mao frying for their misdeeds, but not at all with a baby torn limb from limb in a Planned Parenthood clinic only to be condemned to God's eternal displeasure and judgment. Of course my comfort ultimately has nothing to do with the question except insofar as it stems from being synchronized with the Comforter. But that's why I mention the universal, instinctive desire that children who die be found safe in heaven. The godliest men I know of all have the same desire.

Alice is my daughter; I really want to *know* where she is. Friendly theological banter about abstract concepts moves into another realm when there's a little girl we all loved lying in the churchyard beneath a big black piece of etched granite. I've labored throughout this ordeal to try to understand and face things as they *are*, now how I *want* them to be. That posture has helped greatly in enduring Alice's sickness and death, so I'm hesitant to abandon it.

The issue of the eternal destiny of children is a little complicated, but I'll try to make it simple as I can, though I'm not sure how well I might succeed. The Biblical logic for how a person enters eternity is rather simple, but might lead to a rather difficult conclusion:

1.   All people are sinners by nature from conception. That means that no one is ever morally neutral. (Rom 3:23, 5:12).

2.   The way to be saved from sin's punishment is through faith in Jesus (Acts 16:31).

3.   Everyone who dies not believing in Jesus will be condemned (John 3:18).

4.   Little babies who die didn't believe in Jesus. They couldn't believe in *anything*. Thus, see #3.

The only way to have any biblical assurance that Alice or any little ones who are taken from us will be awaiting us in heaven is to find a way around one of those first three points. And over the course of church history, people have done so in different ways. Some have suggested that children really aren't sinners, so they're "in" because of their innocence. Of course, that might help those who miscarried, but it's harder for me to make the case Alice never sinned, because of course she did. She was wonderful, sure. Perfect? No.

Besides this, another problem is that innocent people don't die; people die *because* they're sinners. Death is the result of sin, that's biblically clear. And if such a thing as an innocent person (besides Jesus) existed, then Jesus dying wasn't really all that necessary and all of us would have a fair shot at it without him.

Let me expand on those three points of biblical logic.

All people are sinners from conception.

The best way I've been able to understand this goes like this: Suppose that dogs are the perfect animal, except for one thing: they bark. I don't think *anybody* is particularly charmed by that sound. I've heard of people playing recordings of babbling brooks or chirping birds to calm themselves or help them fall asleep; *never* have I heard of anyone basking in the mellow sounds of a yipping terrier.

Now let us suppose that heaven is open for all dogs, *except* the ones who bark. (quick aside… as a pastor sometimes I'm asked whether or not dogs will be in heaven. My response is that I'm okay with *my* dog being in heaven, but it would be hell to live next door to *your* dog for all eternity. So in the name of fairness – dogs are out.) Some dogs bark more, some less, some can even be trained to quit barking, but the cold reality is this: dogs are barkers. It's their nature to bark. You can breed them to have different temperaments, to run fast or waddle slowly, to be different colors or have different kinds of hair, but at the end of the day, dogs are barkers. And if you take dogs to heaven without somehow getting the bark out of them, someday a celestial mailman will come walking up to the house, knock on the door, and the barking will commence. Then what?

Is a newborn puppy a barker? Well, yes and no. It's a barker because it's a dog. If it's only 2 minutes old, it's never actually barked, because it doesn't have the cognitive or physical development yet. But give it some time and it'll bark, because it's a dog.

This is at least a little bit what the issue is with sin. Is a newborn a sinner? Well, yes and no. It is by nature, and give it some time, the little angel will prove to have plenty of devil in it. But there's also a really good reason our judicial system treats children differently than adults; we don't put 3 year olds on death row, even if a couple of troublemakers were able to toddle into the missile silo, insert the keys, press the red button, and blow half the world to smithereens. To put it another way, a baby who fills his britches deserves a good change; an ordinary teenager who does the same deserves the joy of doing his own laundry, and maybe a bit of accompanying shame.

So that's the first premise in a simplistic nutshell, *all are sinners*. Assuming little kids don't stay little forever – which they don't – unless something (or Someone) changes their fundamental nature, they'll grow into sinners who sin. And sinners in heaven doesn't work. It would ruin a perfect heaven just the way one sinner, Adam, ruined a perfect earth.

The only way to be saved from sin is through faith in Jesus.

This second premise is basic Bible teaching, and in the early days of the church, that's what was taught. But then people started noticing that babies and kids died. And they died without believing, because they *couldn't* believe. So people started trying to figure a way around this dilemma, because it's difficult to stomach the thought of a nursery in hell.[20] On the other hand, if we just say everybody gets in, then we might as well set the Bible aside and just envision heaven however we desire, because it's pretty clear in there that not everybody gets "in." It's actually a pretty significant dilemma.

Several ways have been proposed to try to get around this: Catholic and Lutheran theologians have proposed salvation through baptism (though they travel different lanes along the same road), others proposed salvation through what is called a Covenant of Grace (in short, the child's parents are believers heading for heaven, so the kids, as long as they are kids, get the same benefits as their parents), some, like my friends, propose salvation through election, meaning God will choose freely to make some (or all) saved before they die, either apart from faith or by giving them faith even though they can't cognitively recognize or exercise it.

But in all these cases, even supposing they work, we're left with the problem of dealing with *un*baptized, *un*covenanted, or *un*elect little ones who are left out in the cold, or more accurately, out in the hot. In the case of the un-elect babies, we might assume they're all chosen, so they're all in, but then, to revisit Luther's doubt, *who really knows*? In the classic case study of twins, Jacob is in heaven, Esau is not, because God chose one and not the other (Romans 9:10-14. That's not a particularly comforting thought in the middle of the night pondering the state of my little ones, believe me. It helps that there *might* be hope, but I'd really like more, please.

Everyone who dies not believing in Jesus will be condemned.

This third premise is the reason I really, really want people to believe in Jesus, because I believe that premise to be true. Believing in Jesus is actually a difficult thing to do,[21] because it means having to take

---

[20] If, as I presume, children who die will be children in heaven, if children who died went to hell it is also presumable they would begin there as children also.

[21] Take the case of the rich young ruler, for example.

what Jesus said seriously, like as seriously as if God said them, because as God, he *did* say them. And He *meant* them. Jesus never really talked just to hear the sound of his own voice. So believing in Jesus means living life under someone else's rules, not my own, and that's a hard pill to swallow. It's far easier to ignore Jesus and pretend like he doesn't have any meaningful authority over how I live my life, or blindly assume he's just pretty happy with me just the way I am. But Jesus knows me too well for that to be true. So anyone can (and many people do) say, "I believe in Jesus," but live as if he is either dead, disinterested, or can be entirely disregarded without consequence. Naturally, nobody lives as if gravity can be disregarded without consequence, at least they don't live very long that way, but many people live that way with regard to Jesus, and he's as real and far more powerful than gravity, and that's going to spell trouble for them.

The Bible is crystal clear: No Jesus, no heaven. Those who depend on him for life will receive it; those who don't, won't. Nobody gets to pretend Jesus' opinion doesn't matter, then expect him to haul us to heaven so he can eternally tolerate our cold shoulder and self-styled way of living. And, to be fair, like having to live next door to a yippy neighbor dog forever, I'd rather not have to live next door to anyone for eternity who is living life by their own rules, and you'd not want to live next door to me following my own rules. Eventually, probably sooner rather than later, if we're all doing our own thing, heaven becomes hell.

So Now What?

The fate of children who die has occupied much of my mind over the course of the last year, even when I found myself so mentally foggy I could scarcely think. I often found myself stammering my way through conversations because my brain couldn't keep up with my tongue, which is the opposite of how it usually goes. It's terrible feeling like the mind doesn't function anymore. That fog is lifting though, thankfully.

The simplest place to begin working my way through the apparent dilemma is with the story of King David having full confidence in seeing his dying little one again in heaven, even though he didn't bother to lay out any reasons why he believed that (2Sam. 12:19-23). One or two extra lines would have been helpful! But in my way of thinking, if his little one made it, others might too, even if I couldn't figure out exactly how.

I decided to write my first seminary paper a couple weeks ago on the fate of children who die. As I studied the reality of sin in all people including children, pondered the holiness of God, and tried rather unsuccessfully to find any meaningful hope in any kind of salvation apart from faith or any meaningful definition of faith apart from the ability to think. I wrestled mightily with all my mind and all my soul and felt crushed by the weight of the heavy, unassailable truths involved. Sin is a big problem, and we've all got it. And even if you were to back up the age of a child until they couldn't commit an *actual* sin, Alice was long past that age. ("Actual sin" is a technical term. Kind of like how a dog is a barker before it actually barks for the first time, at some point every sinner sins for the first time and becomes an actual sinner.)

After spending several days in my office poring over really good books and pondering these matters, my mind weary and shadowed by rather dark and hopeless thoughts, I returned home one night and began walking down our driveway, once again looking up to the stars like I've done a hundred times this past year, thinking about the greatness of God and the smallness of man, and begging Him for some sort of help. I just couldn't understand how Alice could be in heaven without basically making sin meaningless, making faith meaningless, or belittling God's perfect holiness. But the thought of her not being there was so terrible I couldn't make sense of that either. There have been a couple times in my life when, like Jacob, I'm ready to wrestle with God until he blesses me, even if I limp forever. The week I had to watch Alice die was one of those. This was another.

I thought about "all have sinned" and I wrestled with God saying, "Esau have I hated." I thought about how the question of what happens to kids who die revolves around who kids are as human beings. I pondered who God is, and what God does with human beings who are sinners. In some ways, theology is like a giant calculator; you put in the data, add this piece with that one, maybe add one or two other relevant pieces, and come up with a conclusion. Or sometimes the Bible gives a conclusion, and we have to figure out the pieces that lead to the conclusion. It's actually really helpful and necessary and believe me I'm not knocking it. God wrote the Bible in such a way that we could use it to know more about him than is explicitly stated. The frustrating part to me as I wrestled is that God's *judgment* of sin is constant and predictable, but his *mercy* is a bit of a variable and only evident when faith is present. God owes judgment. He doesn't owe mercy. So if there's no reason to assume mercy is present, we can always assume judgment is. That's holiness, and God is holy. The most predictable calculations are not at all in our favor.

The other constant to me was human nature. There's a good reason for that, of course: people are people, and there's no person who is more or less valuable than any other, and that goes for the homeless guy, the billionaire, the great-grandmother whose Alzheimer's is so bad she's of no practical use to society, the bank robber, the genius, the mentally incapacitated 6-year old who will never learn to say his own name, the guy who smoked his brains until they became as intelligent as a head of broccoli, and the fertilized embryo lost behind the ice cream of some laboratory freezer somewhere. Every person is made in God's image, possessing an immortal soul, and going to live somewhere for all eternity, and as such, all equally significant in God's eyes, as they ought to be in ours.

Yet every person is different too. Some are strong, some are weak, some are intellectually gifted, musically gifted, some are insanely, boringly normal, some are heart-breakingly incapacitated and will never have a clue what it even means to be a normal person, much less experience a normal life. In other words, all people are the same, but they're all different. In theology, this is called the person/nature distinction. All persons are equal; all natures are not. Every human being possesses both.

So then I considered how a child's eternal destiny is not determined by an impersonal judge running identical people through a cold mechanical process of theological calculations concluding their eternal state; a child's destiny is personally determined by Judge Jesus, the very same one whose death is the only thing that made it possible for *anyone* to get into heaven, and who said he can give eternal life to whomever he wishes. In other words, if anyone *could* get them into heaven, it'd be him. And he could do so as simultaneously judge and sin-eraser.

So I asked myself, "How could I know what the holy, sinless Jesus did when my precious little sinner stood before him 6 months ago, unable to enter heaven unless he intervened on her behalf?" What does the Bible say? Is there something about Jesus that's predictable enough for me to base my hopes upon? There's one clue that was especially meaningful: children were brought to Jesus, the same Jesus who Alice met, and when the adults tried to pull them away, Jesus said, "*Let the children come to me; do not hinder them, for to such belongs the kingdom of God.*" (Mark 10:14) Then he put his hands on them and blessed them.

The very thought struck me like a bolt of lightning, not in some mystical way, but because it just didn't hit me before: if Jesus said "let them come," who was left to "hinder" them? Sure, Jesus wasn't speaking directly of admitting children into heaven. But he was speaking to them in a different way than he spoke to adults. It is an insight into how God acts toward children. This same Jesus is Alice's judge, and he said, "Let them come!" I've rarely been so happy about anything in my life. For the first time probably since the week she died, I wept. I walked over to my shop, where her radiation mask is hanging off the wall, and little scraps from building her coffin lie scattered about the floor, where pieces of plywood she'd scribbled her name on were leaned up against the table saw, a place I've not been able to enter very often or for very long, and as tears ran down my face, I cried over and over again, "Lord Jesus, you said 'Let them come!' You wouldn't turn her away!'"

Jesus is the judge of my Alice. Sure, she's guilty of being a sinner. As far as I know, she didn't have faith in Jesus any more (and sadly maybe less) than she believed in SpongeBob. She just didn't have the brain-power to understand the gospel yet. I say that as a self-proclaimed Alice authority. I've never studied another person more intently in my life. I'm happy to say I knew her well. I wanted to see some sign of faith in the worst way, believe me. At the end of the day, in a very real and special way, in death she was entirely dependent upon the mercy of the only one who *could* save her *to* save her in that moment, and I happily and confidently trust the one who said, "Let them come."

Michele and I handled all of Alice's affairs in life. Alice never got to say whether or not she would endure radiation or chemo. And you know, she trusted us so implicitly she never questioned us. Those were things beyond her comprehension. We had to make life or death decisions for her, doing so strictly on the basis of our love for her and our understanding of her condition. For our part, we had to trust Jesus with the decision to let her get sick and die, because there are things going on that He's aware of but are beyond our comprehension. So I'm entirely confident that the One making the decisions concerning her eternal destiny on the other side has received her to his arms. That's what he always did and I believe always does with children. It's who He is. Not because she deserved it, but because if he wouldn't receive her, no one else could. He is her only hope. It's a good hope to have.

That's not to say Jesus is unwilling to send people into what he called "outer darkness." Jesus is no teddy bear, which is good, because no teddy bear can defeat sin and raise the dead. In C.S. Lewis' language, the Lion is good, but he's not consequently safe. Jesus did, after all, allow the rich young ruler to ignore his demands and walk away from him and into eternity without him. Hell's population is not zero.

The children though, taken from this world all too soon, Jesus receives to himself, purely by his grace, covering their sins, changing their natures, making them fit to be his own brothers and sisters. Jesus is inclined to mercy; he's not as rigidly unforgiving as mathematics. If you read the wonderful stories in the Bible about Jesus raising people from the dead, I think with the one exception of his friend Lazarus, he always raised children. There's something to that. I long for the day when he stands beside Alice's grave, and says like he once did, *"'Talitha cumi,' which means, 'Little girl, I say to you, arise'"* (Mark 10:14).

When we met with Arlen, the Lewis Lake sexton, to select Alice's gravesite, I also reserved the spot beside Alice for my own grave, and Michele gets the other side of me, so we get front row seats (beds?) for the occasion, and I'm rather excited to see it.

–*jr*

This is from what I think was our last "date," back in mid-April. Everybody was sleeping late except Alice and me, so we snuck out to Nicoll's cafe for breakfast, then to Walmart because she wanted to buy presents for her cousins. Precious minutes, and I wouldn't trade them for anything

Epilogue

Our soul waits for the Lord;
he is our help and our shield.
For our heart is glad in him,
because we trust in his holy name.
Let your steadfast love, O Lord, be upon us,
even as we hope in you.
Psalm 33:20-22

June 14, 2019

Today marks one year since Alice's funeral. We've made the cycle.

I haven't figured out yet why God made life kind of like a spinning tire – going around in circles yet forward at the same time – but the very idea intrigues me. The days leading up to the anniversary (usually such a celebratory word) of Alice's death were difficult for Michele. The days following it have been difficult for me.

The very fact that I can say these last several days have been difficult and you understand why is what's so weird to me: in one sense, we're further from the trauma of the event than we've ever been before so it should be better, yet the cyclical nature of the calendar somehow brings us closer to it than we've been in a long time, so *of course* we're feeling worse.

We often speak of Alice, and although the passage of only a year seems to make her little voice hard to recall or her twinkly eyes difficult to envision without the aid of a photograph, still, once every so often something will jar a memory loose and bring her near once again.

The other night, for instance, we were having our traditional Sunday night popcorn, and Shelly said, "Remember eating popcorn with Alice?" Alice used to love popcorn, but she would only eat it in a certain way. She'd get a bowl of popcorn and a spoon, and come sit in my lap and then we'd eat it together. I have no idea where she got the notion that was the way to do it, but that's just how it was with her, and it was okay by me. Just another one of those little things that made her so endearing. I love those memories when they come popping up.

Several months ago, we received an invitation to a "Day of Remembrance" down at Children's Hospital, to remember all the young patients there who had died in the last year. It was held on June 7th, the day before we would mark one year since Alice's death. We made the drive down, just Shell and I, and as we pulled into that familiar parking ramp in the basement of the hospital, I parked in the same spot I'd parked on our very first visit down; I don't think I'll ever forget that spot, though I'm not sure why.

It was a really strange feeling to be in a place that was so familiar to us without the one person who was always there with us. As we walked up to the door, we talked about how Alice always hit the handicapped access button to open the door. When Alice was with us, we never hit the buttons on the elevator – that was her job too. I'm forty years old and I still like pressing the buttons, must be a country-mouse thing. But it wasn't as fun this time.

We were met almost at the door by our friend Ann, a social worker for the hospital who, among other things, rounded up some paperwork and doctor's signatures to get me relieved from jury duty after I'd been selected while Alice was in radiation. Coincidentally perhaps, I was notified two weeks ago that I've been selected once again, only this time Ann can't help me. But we had a good laugh about it anyway. Ann mentioned how she'd been telling a coworker about Alice and how my brothers and I made her "last bed," (still can't quite say "coffin") and that was pretty amazing because the only way she could have known that is by following our story online from a personal desire to keep up with Alice's story. It spoke volumes about how much she really cared about us and Alice.

We found ourselves in a crowd of people gathered together to commemorate their lost little ones. Ann ushered us into a room filled with tables and chairs and on the tables were little baskets of beads, bells, medallions, along with some ribbons, string, and cookie-shaped slices of a tree. We were invited to make a little work of art from these things, so I grabbed a red ribbon, Shelly wrote Alice's name on the wood, and we put together some beads and bells, and went to the service.

I didn't count how many names were read, but I would imagine it was thirty-five or so. As they displayed the pictures of each one of these little ones, I noticed that some had troubles which were plainly evident and some, like Alice, had troubles that weren't. From preemies to teenagers, covering about every major ethnicity from Hispanic to Asian to American Indian, we witnessed a steady stream of teary-eyed parents walking forward as their child's name was announced to hang their little work of art on this tree. I took my turn as well. It was quite moving, to say the least. We realized yet again that we are not alone in our sorrow.

Afterwards Dr. Tammie and Dr. G. came up to give us each a big hug and visit with us, and we loved it so very much as they spoke with great fondness and love for her. It's a wonderful thing to have your child honored by people of their rank and abilities. We're so grateful for them.

The next day was Saturday, the anniversary of Alice's death. Michele had planned a little family get-together at the cemetery, and Alice's four grandparents and a pile of aunts, uncles, and cousins met us out there. I was helping Pastor Bob do a leadership retreat that morning, but he graciously released me for part of it to meet with the family.

We didn't really plan out what we'd do, so we all gathered around and more or less choked out Psalm 23. The volume was pretty awful considering there were about thirty of us there, but it was appropriately awful, since it mostly meant we couldn't quite speak. I asked my Dad to pray and he gave thanks for Alice, testified of our continuing trust in God's plans, and asked Him to help us endure. One of my sisters-in-law brought a whole bunch of red balloons, and since my brother Keith is the fun uncle, I asked him to orchestrate the launch. So the kids launched them, just like they did at her funeral. How cool to see them all go flying off into the wild blue. Violet, for her part, decided to hang on to hers and play with it for a bit before finally wanting to send it off.

I always took a good family for granted; I don't know what it's like not to have a wonderful family. Only in recent years have I begun to learn how valuable a gift that is. And though we've been through some hard stuff, I'm so grateful that we've gone through almost all of it together. Good parents, good siblings, good nieces & nephews, and good in-laws. Pretty awesome.

Sunday morning at Lewis Lake we were greeted by so many people wearing Alice t-shirts. They haven't forgotten, and once again, I felt the joy that comes from those I love honoring my Alice. While I can't even imagine *exactly* how the Heavenly Father feels when His Son is honored, I think I do understand it a little better now than I did before. Yet one more of the many valuable lessons I've learned via Alice. They're still not all worth losing her yet, and the tears that regularly and randomly trickle down my dear wife's face are a stark reminder of that reality, but in a small, limited way we're beginning to see that lousy stuff can be worked for good.

I still look forward to that future day when we will hold our Alice and say, "I'm totally glad this went down the way it did!" Still, to quote Aragorn, "Today is not that day!" But then, as my dear friend Vasiliy likes to say in his heavy Russian accent, "What we can do man? We don't have any one choice!" Which is true. This is the path we have been given to walk, and walk it we must. But then he also likes to say, "If God helps, we can."

So, as we said at the beginning: God help us. Or, to borrow a line from Dickens' Tiny Tim, that particularly charming crippled child whose special relationship to his Daddy strikes me so powerfully whenever I reflect on it because it so beautifully paralleled the relationship between Alice and me, "God bless us, every one!"

Joe Reed is a native of Grand Rapids Michigan and raised in Northern Minnesota. He earned his bachelor's degree from Cornerstone University in 2002 and is currently pursuing an MDiv at Southern Baptist Theological Seminary. Joe is Associate Pastor at Lewis Lake Covenant Church in Ogilvie, MN, and resides in nearby Rock Creek with his wife Michele and five children.

Made in the USA
San Bernardino, CA
25 June 2019